I0797801

35 Natural Wonders in Georgia to See before You Die

35 Natural Wonders in Georgia to See before You Die

Ann Litrel and Charles Seabrook

The University of Georgia Press — ATHENS

This publication is made possible in part through a grant from the Bruce and Georgia McEver Fund for the Arts and Environment.

Athens, Georgia 30602
www.ugapress.org

Designed by Erin Kirk
Set in Warnock Pro
Printed and bound by Sheridan Books
The paper in this book meets the guidelines for permanence and durability of the Committee on Production Guidelines for Book Longevity of the Council on Library Resources.

Most University of Georgia Press titles are available from popular e-book vendors.

Printed in the United States of America
29 28 27 26 25 C 5 4 3 2 1

Library of Congress Cataloging-in-Publication Data

Names: Litrel, Ann, 1964– author | Seabrook, Charles author
Title: 35 natural wonders of Georgia to see before you die / Ann Litrel and Charles Seabrook.
Other titles: Thirty-five natural wonders of Georgia to see before you die
Description: Athens : The University of Georgia Press, [2025]
Identifiers: LCCN 2025020255 | ISBN 9780820374444 hardback
Subjects: LCSH: Litrel, Ann, 1964—Travel | Natural areas—Georgia—Guidebooks | Natural monuments—Georgia—Guidebooks | Natural history—Georgia—Guidebooks | Georgia—Description and travel
Classification: LCC F284.3 .L58 2025 | DDC 917.5804—dcundefined
LC record available at https://lccn.loc.gov/2025020255

Contents

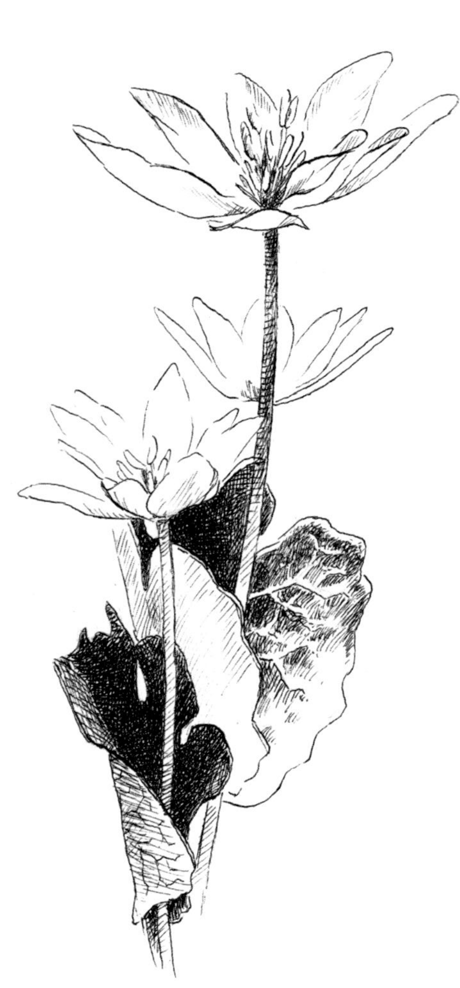

Preface

I needed a list.

A decade of painting picturesque farms and landmarks around my hometown of Woodstock found me ready to venture beyond Cherokee County. After some thought, I decided to paint Georgia's most beautiful nature spots. The phrase "natural wonders" came to mind.

An internet search yielded an intriguing list, "35 Natural Wonders in Georgia to See before You Die." It was a bucket list by Charles Seabrook, long-time columnist for the *Atlanta Journal-Constitution*. His descriptions leaped off the screen, with nicknames like Georgia's Amazon for the Altamaha River and Little Grand Canyon for Providence Canyon. Many were unfamiliar to me—Ebenezer Creek, Graves Mountain, Broxton Rocks.

What a great list, I thought. *My next project. I'll travel the state and paint a picture of each place*. My conservative estimate for the project was two to three years—a typical time line for my past painting collections.

It was an ambush. Charlie's list knocked me off my feet. Each wonder, from Cumberland Island to Brasstown Bald, was rich, beautiful, and incredibly diverse with life. I saw that I could spend two to three years painting just one site. The scope of the project swelled. To complicate matters, some spots were proving a challenge to explore and learn about.

I thought maybe Mr. Seabrook might be willing to help. I introduced myself through an email, and we arranged to meet for lunch.

It may have been our first meeting, but it was clear that Charlie had never met a stranger. We shared a common interest in the natural world, and we quickly agreed that many Georgians—like me before "the list"—don't know what a treasure trove of natural beauty and diversity Georgia holds. Charlie launched into a story.

"I just visited a friend whose daughter came back from biology research in Costa Rica. The daughter was enthusiastically telling us all about Costa Rica's native hummingbirds. There were fifty-four species, and she knew all their names, how to identify them.

"And then, as we were talking, she looked out the window beside us and noticed a bird outside on a tree. 'What kind of bird is that!?' she asked. She was very interested, having just gotten back from her project."

Charlie smiled. "Well, it was a tufted titmouse!—one of the most common birds in all of Georgia. And then she asked, 'So what kind of tree is that?'"

He laughed. "Here she'd just spent two months memorizing dozens of birds in another country, and she didn't know one of the most common birds in her home state of Georgia, perched on one of the most common trees—a dogwood."

Charlie said this not with the bite of a critic but more with the smile of a philosopher, ruefully noting the state of the world.

"So what are you trying to do again?" he asked, as our lunch conversation wound to a close.

"Well, I feel like people have this idea that 'nature' is somewhere else—out west in a national park or in the Amazon. But they miss the nature right in our backyard. I want to paint what's around us right here in Georgia—so people actually see it!"

Charlie shook my hand encouragingly as we left the restaurant and promised to help. "Keep it up! It's a worthwhile effort!"

Five years passed from my discovery of the list. I had traveled and painted from one corner of Georgia to the other; I had yet to visit four of the thirty-five wonders. But it now seemed to me that this list of miraculous places was deserving of more than beautiful paintings. The Georgia Natural Wonders project needed to be a book—and Charlie, the author of the list, needed to write it.

Once again I invited Charlie to meet over lunch. This time I would pitch the book: *Georgia Natural Wonders* would have two voices—the artist, inviting the reader to see each place for the first time through story and paintings. And Charlie, the journalist and science writer, sharing his lifetime of knowledge, illuminating the multitude of reasons that make each place a wonder.

The lunch ended with Charlie's enthusiastic agreement. "Well, I've been working on another book . . . but your idea intrigues me. You've convinced me!"

And that was how this book came to be.

Georgia Natural Wonders is not a travel guide or a list of outfitters and guides. These things come and go. The book is a tribute to what is enduring in Georgia—its marvelous natural wonders, the diversity of its life and the land, and how these places came to be.

—A. L.

I've been writing a popular weekly column called "Wild Georgia" for the *Atlanta Journal-Constitution* since September 1994—a commentary on the weekly passing of the natural year and on nature's great handiwork in the Peach State. I usually reserve Mondays to write the column and most of the time have at least a notion of what I'll write about.

But on a Monday in late January 2008, when I sat down at my desk to write, the words would not come to me. I had a writer's greatest fear—writer's block. For a long time, I sat in my cramped office trying to come up with a fresh idea or a new approach to an old topic. For inspiration, I scanned the titles of the books in a bookcase next to my desk, and that's when I saw it—the book *1,000 Places to See before You Die*, by Patricia Schultz. The book was part of a trend at the time. Lists that suggested things you should do, see, read, taste, or listen to before you die were everywhere.

And the idea hit me: I would compile my own before-you-die list, a list of what I was most familiar with, natural places in Georgia. I was reenergized, and my writer's block vanished. I quickly began jotting down a list of such places and in short order had well more than fifty. I spent the rest of the day revising, trimming, adding to, and repeatedly going over the list. I contacted some naturalist friends who knew Georgia's natural areas as well as anybody and asked for their suggestions. At the end of the day, I had a list of thirty-five natural wonders that I would recommend as places to see during one's lifetime. In all honesty, I was limited to thirty-five because that's all I could fit into the space for my column.

On February 3, 2008, the *Atlanta Journal-Constitution* published the "Wild Georgia" column containing my list with a one-sentence description of each place. I hoped—as I always do—that it would get a good reception from readers, who might be inspired to get out into Georgia's great outdoors and see these places. I was flabbergasted, however, at the tremendous response I got. Reader after reader told me they had clipped the column and taped it to their refrigerator doors and tacked it to kitchen message boards to use as their bucket list for visiting Georgia's wild places. Over the years, the favorable responses kept trickling in.

Indeed, a particularly gratifying response came several years after I shared the list. Ann Litrel, an accomplished artist in Woodstock, reached me by email and said that not only was she visiting all thirty-five places, she also was painting each of them. A lunch followed and she told me that she eventually planned to have a gallery showing of her works. At a second lunch, she revealed her plan for a book to showcase her art. I readily agreed to add my comments on why these places deserve special recognition. The result is the book you now hold in your hand. The thirty-five natural places are its chapters.

Coming up with my list within a short time to meet a deadline was not an easy task—but not because Georgia has few natural places to pick from. The difficulty was that Georgia is blessed with an abundance of natural diversity and splendor, which made it tougher to decide what should appear on the list.

Georgia, in fact, has an incredibly diverse natural richness. With about 4,440 species of native plants and animals, Georgia ranks sixth among all the states in biodiversity, according to the Nature Conservancy. As the authors of the 2013 book *Natural Communities of Georgia* note: "From cool mountain peaks in the Blue Ridge to the sun-drenched shores of our Atlantic coast, this state boasts an amazing diversity of natural habitats. This diversity of habitats supports an equally impressive variety of plant and animal communities."

About one hundred such habitats, ranging from mountain ridge forests and deep caverns to coastal salt marshes and bottomland hardwood swamps, exist in Georgia—wild places where certain groups of plants and animal species prefer to live.

More than two hundred species of trees are native to Georgia, more than half the number in all of Europe. Birdwatchers have seen and recorded about four hundred bird species in the state. Of these, 322 species make regular appearances in the Peach State. This tremendous variety of life also extends to other native wild creatures—mammals, snakes, salamanders, frogs, freshwater and saltwater fish and mammals, insects, and on and on. Seventy of the state's native species are on the federal list of endangered and threatened species.

Such amazing diversity is mainly the result of Georgia's five physiogeographic regions—the Appalachian (or Cumberland) Plateau; Ridge and Valley Region; Blue Ridge Mountains; Piedmont; and Coastal Plain. All differ in geology, topography, soil, and climate. For instance, the seasonal climate on North Georgia's mountain summits may be similar to that of some northeastern states'; the climate of coastal barrier islands resembles subtropical climates. Georgia also is fortunate to have two great national forests—the 750,000-acre Chattahoochee National Forest stretching across most of North Georgia and the 116,000-acre Oconee National Forest in Middle Georgia.

For my thirty-five places, I chose representatives of all five regions. I picked them not only because of their outstanding beauty but also because they represent various types of habitats and ecosystems—swamps, hardwood forests, rivers, mountain peaks, sandhills, and such. Some were obvious choices. The vast Okefenokee Swamp and the magnificent Cumberland Island National Seashore, for instance, belong on anyone's list of natural places to visit. Some, however, are not so well known, such as Graves Mountain, the outstanding geologic treasure in Lincoln County, and the rare prairie habitats of Oaky Woods in Houston County. Most of the places are publicly accessible, but some, such as the Wade Tract in Thomas County, are privately owned and require special permission to visit. Readers also may have their own candidates for a list of Georgia's natural wonders.

In addition to her art, Ann has written short essays on seeing each of these places through the eyes of an artist and as someone seeing them—at least most of them—for the first time. In separate essays, I describe the geology, biology, ecology, and other natural features that come together to make these places so special, places that one should see before dying.

—C. S.

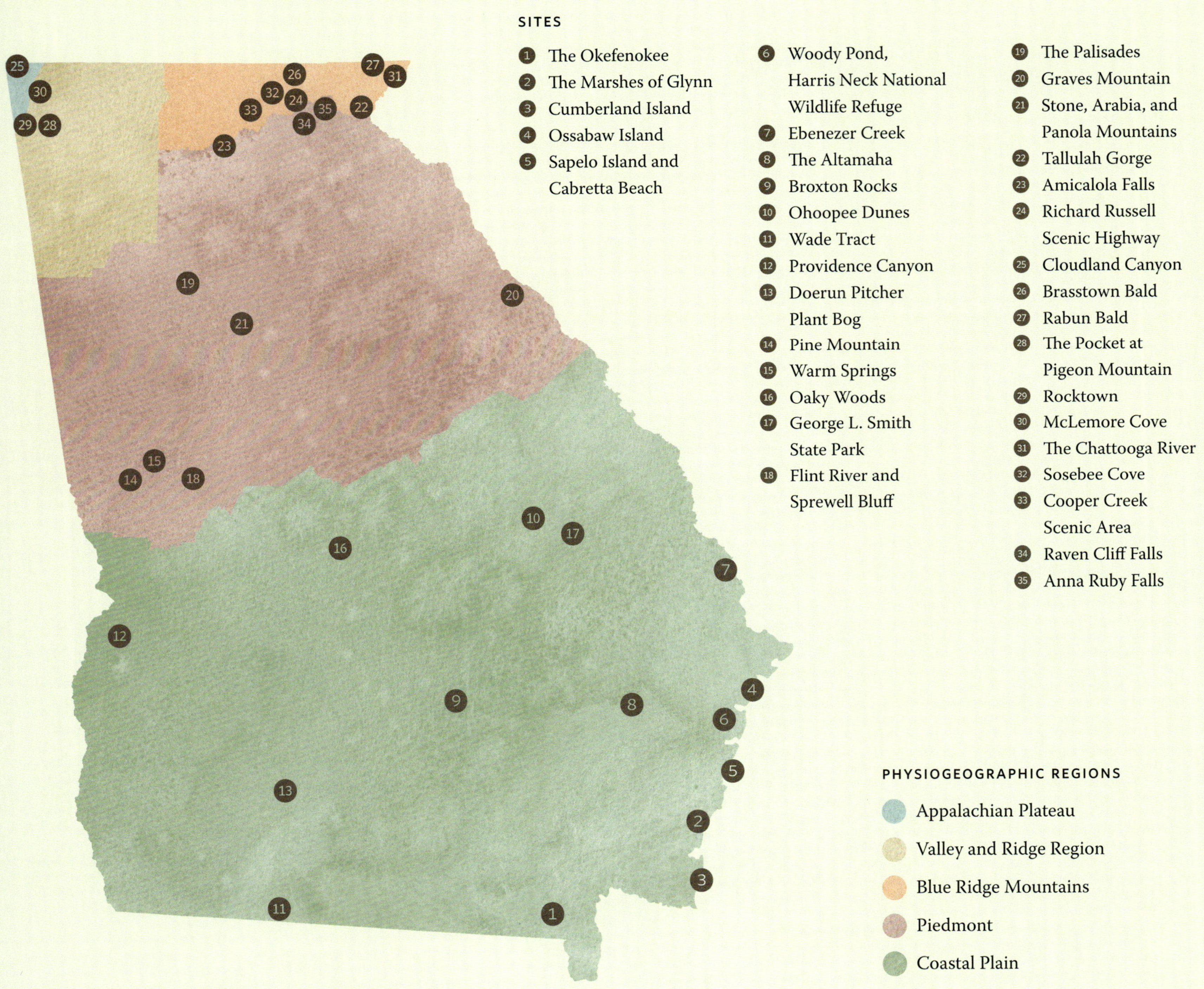
SITES
1 The Okefenokee
2 The Marshes of Glynn
3 Cumberland Island
4 Ossabaw Island
5 Sapelo Island and Cabretta Beach
6 Woody Pond, Harris Neck National Wildlife Refuge
7 Ebenezer Creek
8 The Altamaha
9 Broxton Rocks
10 Ohoopee Dunes
11 Wade Tract
12 Providence Canyon
13 Doerun Pitcher Plant Bog
14 Pine Mountain
15 Warm Springs
16 Oaky Woods
17 George L. Smith State Park
18 Flint River and Sprewell Bluff
19 The Palisades
20 Graves Mountain
21 Stone, Arabia, and Panola Mountains
22 Tallulah Gorge
23 Amicalola Falls
24 Richard Russell Scenic Highway
25 Cloudland Canyon
26 Brasstown Bald
27 Rabun Bald
28 The Pocket at Pigeon Mountain
29 Rocktown
30 McLemore Cove
31 The Chattooga River
32 Sosebee Cove
33 Cooper Creek Scenic Area
34 Raven Cliff Falls
35 Anna Ruby Falls
PHYSIOGEOGRAPHIC REGIONS
Appalachian Plateau
Valley and Ridge Region
Blue Ridge Mountains
Piedmont
Coastal Plain

35 Natural Wonders in Georgia to See before You Die

1 The Okefenokee

North America's largest blackwater swamp, an alligator haven

Murky waters, curtains of moss, and plenty of alligators. My picture of a swamp was a childhood impression of a shadowy bayou, formed, I suspect, by an old Scooby-Doo cartoon.

I was about to be enlightened.

Number 1 on the list of Georgia natural wonders is Okefenokee Swamp, the largest freshwater swamp east of the Mississippi. It lies in the desolate flatlands of southeastern Georgia, fifty miles from the sea (just south of Waycross and east of Valdosta). I enlisted my adventure-loving sister Jane as a travel companion and booked us a guided three-day kayak trip, during which we and the other members of our group would ferry our supplies in our boats and camp each night on platforms raised above the swamp waters.

As it turned out, I was right about the alligators. We saw them every hour. Everywhere.

But we also had surprises.

Our guide, Sheila Willis, was a piece of living history—a self-proclaimed "swamper" whose family had lived in the trackless wetland going back almost two hundred years. Sixty years old, she is a member of the last generation to know many of the old settler stories, a trove of tales she shared with us about life in the swamp as it once was.

OPPOSITE: *Sky and water at Okefenokee seemed to merge, with the shapes of the living plants and people floating between them, ephemeral and passing. In this painting I allowed the blues to seep into the trees and boaters to show the infinite pervasiveness of that sky and water.*

As she led our kayaks through the maze of water trails, she often stopped us to point out countless strange bird calls and name the source of each. In one instance, she pulled up to a hummock where she stripped some leaves from a bush, wetted and crushed them, and opened her hands to show us the lather from poor man's soap (*Clethra alnifolia*).

The water, too, was a surprise—not at all murky but translucent like dark tea, making the surface a perfect mirror that dazzled us from the moment of our morning launch. Our laden kayaks entered a mile of engineered canal, and we paddled silently through a tunnel of overhanging trees, their perfect reflections lending our progress the unearthly effect of traveling through a wormhole. We looked on in wonder, snapping endless pictures, futilely trying to capture the perfection of an elusive world that existed only as reflected beneath the real.

Leaving the straightway of the canal by midmorning, we followed Sheila through a maze of shadowy trees draped with moss (indeed like curtains). We emerged at midday in another surprise—what is known as a swamp prairie: a wide field of water with undulating borders of water lilies, immense clusters massed in a wavy carpet of leaves under the sun. In open waters, the dome of the sky was reflected in the perfect mirror below, a deeper blue, another world with its own clouds moving like those overhead.

We set up our tents that night on a raised platform above the water and then savored the view. I took the opportunity to sketch. Sheila expertly prepared our hot meal on the camp stove while waving away our offers of help. I walked along the narrow spit of solid ground adjoining our platform and sat on a dry spot to draw a view of our campsite and the pink light frosting the gray, mossy trees. As night fell, the darkness was utter, the stars shining bright in the wilderness sky.

OPPOSITE: *I was surprised to find the swamp as much a world of light as of shadow. Here the luminous blooms of yellow coreopsis float above deep midday shadows. Dark runs of paint suggest reflections trailing down into the mirror of the water.*

A water lily glimmers in the November sun, each translucent petal painted separately to capture the delicately shifting hues reflected from surrounding skies and water.

A roaring bellow jolted us awake at dawn. The sound seemed to come from somewhere close to our platform. We peered through the tent flap. No alligator was in sight, but we heard Sheila's voice beside us confirming it was indeed a bull alligator sounding its territorial call. We kept an eye out during breakfast for our unseen neighbor but didn't spot another alligator until Jane and I launched our kayak for the day's explorations. As we paddled through a narrow channel, a ten-footer slid from the grasses into the water just in front of us.

I felt Jane lurch behind me just as I did, and in unspoken agreement we frantically strained to stop our boat from crossing the alligator's path. We knew he must be in the water just ahead of us. We called anxiously to Sheila behind us. She paddled up with nonchalance, glanced at the tea-tinted shallows, and said, "Looks like he has enough room down there to stay out of your way. Go ahead."

The real Okefenokee was not at all what I had imagined. Yes, it has moss-draped trees and alligators but also night skies full of stars, shining white egrets perched in watchtower trees, and healthy waters alive with fish and turtles and frogs.

On our final afternoon, the swamp offered us the gift of Chesser Prairie in the golden hour before sunset. As Sheila made camp for the evening, Jane and I paddled alone out into the lanes of blue water, now separated by blooming islands of golden coreopsis ablaze in the dying days of November's Indian summer. We paused to watch a lone monarch butterfly stop for nectar before hurrying along his journey south for winter.

After dinner, at sunset, like an unexpected benediction, unfamiliar bird cries came rippling across the grass to our platform. Sheila pulled out her binoculars to let us look—and there, heads and necks bobbing above the marsh grasses, were four sandhill cranes, settling down for their evening roost in the shallow water. As the sun set, we slept in the peace of a still-untouched wilderness.

—A. L.

OPPOSITE: *Chesser Prairie in November was a blaze of yellow coreopsis blooms. Reflected below is the mirror of sky and clouds, painted here as it appeared to me—as real as the world above.*

The prairie's tangle of grasses and flowers is rendered in the exacting precision of pen and ink, with a counterpoint of only loosely painted washes to suggest the late afternoon sunlight on the trees and passing butterfly.

If one were limited to visiting only one natural treasure in Georgia, the vast Okefenokee should be it. Few of the world's other great wetlands can match it. It has been called the prince of southern swamps, and the National Park Service has declared it a National Natural Landmark. Over the years, I've visited the astoundingly beautiful 438,000-acre Okefenokee numerous times—all parts of it, from its bottomland forests and sun-drenched prairies to its floating islands and lakes of mirror-smooth, inky blackwater. I've stepped onto its floating islands of peat and decaying plants that quiver, jellylike, beneath my feet—like walking on a backyard trampoline. It's why the Seminoles and Creeks called it the "land of the trembling earth." It all takes my breath away.

Most of the wetland lies within the confines of the Okefenokee National Wildlife Refuge, managed by the U.S. Fish and Wildlife Service. In 1974 more than 350,000 acres in the refuge were designated a national wilderness area, the highest form of federal protection for an ecosystem.

Geologically, the Okefenokee is young. It was formed over the past sixty-five hundred years by the buildup of carbon-storing peat in a shallow basin on the edge of an ancient Atlantic Ocean coastal terrace—the leftover of a Pleistocene estuary from the time when the ocean covered that part of Georgia. Bordering the eastern side of the swamp is Trail Ridge, a wide strip of elevated land believed to have formed from ancient coastal dunes or an offshore barrier island. The ridge acts as a natural dam for the Okefenokee. Without the ridge, the rainfall-fed swamp would not exist in its current splendor. Two rivers, the Suwannee and the St. Marys—exceptionally beautiful in their own right—rise in the Okefenokee. The St. Marys flows into the Atlantic, the Suwannee into the Gulf of Mexico.

Some people view swamps as dark, shadowy, and mysterious, metaphors for moral decadence. But to nature lovers like me, swamps are magical, redolent of fecundity, rich in wildlife—places of peace, tranquility, and otherworldly beauty.

My spirit soars when I gaze at the Okefenokee's towering pond cypresses (*Taxodium ascendens*) with ramrod-straight trunks flaring out at the bottom in swollen buttresses often surrounded by small, peculiar pointy "knees"—all reflected in the dark swamp water. Pond cypresses (cousins of bald cypresses) are the swamp's dominant trees, casting an enchanting aura over the great wetland. Draped in Spanish moss, they may be eighty feet tall or more and older than four hundred years. A special trait, rot resistance, makes the cypresses appealing for making furniture and other wood products.

If the pond cypress is the swamp's signature tree, its most common—and most dramatic—wildflower is the fragrant, white-flowered water lily, which floats in large masses on the swamp's reflective waters in spring.

Spring brings out other great floral beauty. The swamp's grassy prairie regions become lush with the strikingly beautiful golden club, one of the swamp's more common aquatic wildflowers. Old-timers say that when the golden club blooms, it is truly spring in the Okefenokee. The plant has minute, golden-yellow flowers clustered at the tip of a spike. Below the yellow tip, the spike is white, then red. A waxy coating on the leaves repels water and gives the plant its nickname, "neverwet."

Also abundant in spring are the eye-catching purple-blue blooms of the swamp iris. Butterworts, bladderworts, and sundews—all insect-eating plants—cast more sparkle. In addition, three species of carnivorous pitcher plants—yellow trumpet, hooded, and parrot—add mystery and strangeness to the swamp.

In all, more than six hundred plant species, an amazing number, are native to the Okefenokee.

Making the swamp world renowned, though, is its diverse fauna. An enumeration of its more than 440 species of vertebrate animals shows 39 fishes, 37 amphibians, 64 reptiles, 235 birds, and 50 mammals. They include eleven endangered or threatened species such as the red-cockaded woodpecker and the flatwoods salamander. But its most famous denizen is the American alligator. Gators are ubiquitous in the swamp, the creatures that most people associate with the vast wetland. An estimated twelve thousand gators reside in the swamp, sunning on banks or swimming ever so slowly among lily pads—all the while remaining seemingly oblivious to human visitors. Like all of the Okefenokee's other inhabitants, the crafty gators add their own spellbinding magic to the swamp.

Invertebrate species, however, surpass by magnitudes the number of creatures with backbones. As you would expect, as a swamp the Okefenokee is home to countless native insect species—collectively crucial to nutrient recycling in the swamp. As much as 40 percent of the wetland's forest canopy is consumed by insects and their larvae, particularly the caterpillars of moths and butterflies. Roughly one thousand moth species have been found in the swamp.

Because of all this, the Okefenokee refuge is on the global list of places being considered for designation as a UNESCO World Heritage Site. (UNESCO stands for United Nations Educational, Scientific, and Cultural Organization.) The title is reserved for places on Earth that are of outstanding universal value to humanity and, as such, are to be protected for future generations to appreciate and enjoy. The Okefenokee deserves it.

What it does not deserve are the seemingly endless human threats to its fragile health and ecological integrity. For decades, loggers, miners, and developers have desired a piece of the great swamp for quick profits. There have been, for example, proposals to strip-mine Trail Ridge at the eastern edge of the swamp. Scientists and ecologists have repeatedly warned of the risks to the Okefenokee's intricate hydrology (or natural plumbing). If the swamp's hydrology is disrupted, the damage could endanger the well-being of the entire swamp. The vast wetland could cease to exist as we know it now.

Come see this magnificent place for yourself and why multitudes of people vow to protect it.

—C. S.

2 The Marshes of Glynn

Boundless salt marsh, nursery for coastal life

I've seen the Marshes of Glynn scores of times when crossing the spare but lovely landscape on the causeways connecting Georgia's barrier islands and beaches to the mainland. The Marshes of Glynn, on Highway 17 in Glynn County, have been a constant, wild and beautiful—but always the sideshow, not the main event.

Now, I have spent a week traveling these marshes with Charlie Seabrook—or, at least, traveling with him through the pages of his book *The World of the Salt Marsh*. I have learned that the ebb and flow of the tides through the marsh are the lifeblood of the coast; that the marshes serve as a nursery for most of Georgia's seafood species, including oysters, shrimp, and fish.

In short, the marshes form the foundation for life along Georgia's coast.

My husband has a favorite expression. As a surgeon, he mentors younger doctors, and he sometimes quips, "The eyes don't see what the mind don't know." That is, if you don't know the anatomy of what's in front of you, you won't recognize it when you see it.

Charlie's book illuminated the anatomy of the salt marsh for me, tracing its complex interconnections with all of life on the coast. What will I see now when I return?

OPPOSITE: *The reflection of marsh grass and sky fades into the white of the paper, flowing past its edges to evoke the boundless space that characterizes the wetland. The forms of the white ibis, fishing in the shallows of the Marshes of Glynn, create the sole movement in this quiet scene.*

It's the hour before sunrise, and I am passing through the marshes on Highway 17, approaching the causeway to St. Simons Island. I park at Marshes of Glynn Overlook Park and wait for the sun, looking over the marsh in the dim light before dawn. The sky lightens. The clouds pull apart, and the morning sun leaps out to spread its light over the green marsh grasses waving under the sky. I'm pulled into this great wide space, unburdened of worry and everyday matters.

I decide to spend the morning at Earth Day Nature Trail, just a couple miles away. It seems the ideal spot to see the marsh anew. The trail is short and the park small. Yet I know now how much can be present where it might seem as if nothing is there at all.

I cross the short boardwalk and meander along the loop trail on a tiny marsh hammock. Everywhere, the fertile plants of the marsh edge present their gifts—eastern cedar's blue berries, the red of native holly. St. John's wort blossoms in bright yellow, and sea oxeye daisy stares dark brown from its ring of golden petals.

Across a channel, on the next small hammock, a big great blue heron eyes me from the branches of a cedar, turning his glowing yellow eye in my direction. I cross the boardwalk to get closer but am waylaid by a flurry of movement, a half-dozen ibises eagerly fishing the watery flats on either side of me. They poke and prod in the dull gray mud. My mind's eye now supplies what is too small to be seen from my vantage point—the untold numbers of fiddlers and crabs, insects and worms abundant in the mud of this fertile marsh.

I make my way to the edge of the next hammock and find a dry spot to sit. The aroma of salt air and decaying matter assails my nostrils with the briny tang of the marsh—hydrogen sulfide gas from the bacteria living here. Clumps of grass merge into a wave of green across the marsh—this is the salt-tolerant *Spartina alterniflora*, also called smooth cordgrass. I focus on the clump closest to me that's protruding from the muddy flat. Beneath, I know its roots join a huge network that protects the marsh from storm surges and waves. Tiny sparkles appear on the grass stems—flecks of salt ejected by the plant through glands in its blades. This is just one of the adaptations of cordgrass for its life in this harsh saltwater home. Also on the grass are pale gray periwinkles (tiny snails) clinging to the blades. They will inch their way endlessly up and down the stems with the tide, eating the algae fed by the sun and the waters of this great marsh. Around the grass, raccoon tracks scribble across the mud, and fiddler crabs scuttle, aimlessly waving their big claws as they dip into the mud, eating tiny bits of fungus, algae, and decaying plant and animal matter.

I've passed this marsh so many times—a Georgia island honeymoon long ago, visits with friends and family over the decades, and with our children, now grown. I've delighted in the birds, sampled the breeze, and drunk deep of the vistas.

I've always seen a beautiful painting, wide and full of light, the blue sky and water, the green grasses. It is that painting still.

But knowledge has bestowed this gift—I see now, beneath the blue and the green, a creation even more beautiful: deeply layered, intricately textured, and etched with the infinite and interconnected lines of the web of life.

—A. L.

The Marshes of Glynn were the realm of Georgia's most revered poet, Sidney Lanier, whose deep, passionate writing in the late nineteenth century was inspired by the state's superb natural beauty. His most cherished poem, "The Marshes of Glynn," immortalized the grand, sweeping salt marshes that occupy nearly a third of the coastal county of that name.

Written in 1878, the poem is an epiphanic journey into "the length and the breadth and the sweep of the marshes of Glynn." Perhaps no other literary work captures the beauty, spirit, and grandeur of the salt marsh. In essence, he eloquently tells of having a kind of revelation as he ponders—from the edge of a forest—the great expanse of marsh spreading before him as far as the eye can see:

Oh, what is abroad in the marsh and the terminal sea?
  Somehow my soul seems suddenly free
From the weighing of fate and the sad discussion of sin,
By the length and the breadth and the sweep of the
  marshes of Glynn.
Ye marshes, how candid and simple and nothing-
  withholding and free
Ye publish yourselves to the sky and offer yourselves
  to the sea!
("The Marshes of Glynn," lines 61–66)

With such verses, Lanier, who was suffering from a fatal case of tuberculosis when he wrote the poem, used the marshes to understand the majesty of God's creations while soothing his own body and soul. As his vision expands seaward, he recognizes in an enlightening moment that the marshes and sea, in their vastness, are the expression of "the greatness of God" and are filled with power and mystery.

Generations of Georgia schoolchildren have committed passages of the poem to memory. For more than a century, they and others who have read Lanier's work have come to Georgia's coast to see the majestic natural system that so enraptured the poet, perhaps wondering if they, too, would have an epiphany. Like Lanier, countless visitors have come to realize that the marshes are places of breathtaking beauty, where "a world of marsh that borders a world of sea" can uplift and refresh the human spirit.

Onshore vantage points on Jekyll Island, St. Simons Island, and an overlook park in the city of Brunswick offer magnificent views of the seemingly boundless marshes of Glynn, which resemble a midwestern tall-grass prairie or a vast suburban lawn neatly trimmed by a giant mower. About 90 percent of the muddy landscape is densely covered by a single species, smooth cordgrass. Sparkling tidal creeks and rivers twist through the great marsh as if for the pure joy of it. The creeks and rivers flow into a wide estuary known as St. Simons Sound, abundant with marine life, that connects directly to the sea.

Together, the spacious marshes, broad estuary, tidal streams, and verdant islands make up a landscape of unsurpassed beauty.

A league and a league of marsh-grass, waist-high,
  broad in the blade,
Green, and all of a height, and unflecked with a light
  or a shade,
Stretch leisurely off, in a pleasant plain,
To the terminal blue of the main.
("The Marshes of Glynn," lines 57–60)

Also unequaled is the importance of the salt marsh as an ecosystem. The waving fields of live cordgrass are like nurseries, sheltering young marine creatures from predators. When the cordgrass dies, bacteria, fungi, and other microbes transform it into a highly nutritious food called detritus. The organic matter feeds countless marine organisms in the estuaries, rivers, and creeks—including 75 to 80 percent of the shrimp, blue crabs, and other economically important shellfish species found along the coast. Altogether, Georgia's salt marshes remarkably yield nearly twenty tons of biomass per acre—four times more than the most carefully cultivated farmland.

The pulsing heart of this great ecosystem is the tides. Twice-a-day surges of six to nine feet high—the highest in the Southeast—push saltwater from the sea into the estuaries and then into the tidal creeks that distribute the water throughout the marsh. Sidney Lanier described it this way:

> Look how the grace of the sea doth go
> About and about through the intricate channels that flow
> Here and there,
> Everywhere.
> ("The Marshes of Glynn," lines 81–84)

The incoming tide ferries all manner of marine life into the marsh, as well as nutrients and sediments that nourish the cordgrass. The outgoing tide transports the detritus and other organic matter out of the marsh and into the creeks, rivers, and estuaries.

But the marshes' free services don't end there. They protect the mainland from storm surges, filter out pollutants, and maintain the physical integrity of the barrier islands.

No wonder, then, that Sidney Lanier was uplifted and moved to exultation as he reverently contemplated the "liberal marshes of Glynn." His marshes are still there, still inspiring joy and wonder in multitudes of others.

—C. S.

3 Cumberland Island

A wealth of wildlife and grandeur, nature and history

My sister Jane describes a night of camping under the stars at Cumberland Island National Seashore, Georgia's southernmost sea island; a coworker recounts taking the ferry to see the wild horses; a neighbor tells of watching baby loggerhead turtles hatch on the beach.

Stories about Cumberland Island have followed me since I moved to Georgia. Yet somehow, in three decades, I had never managed a visit. March 2017 was the turning point. I was searching online for ideas—some authoritative reference—to guide my next series of paintings, and that was when I came across Charlie Seabrook's 2008 column "35 Natural Wonders in Georgia to See before You Die" (see the preface). His bucket list followed a rambling course across the state, starting in the southeast corner. I was delighted: he included places I'd never heard of. But there, in the number 3 spot, sat Cumberland Island.

The list launched the next seven years of my life as an artist.

I called my friend Ginger the next week. Would she like to come with me to Cumberland Island? Her answer was an emphatic *yes*.

Cumberland Island is immense and wild—bigger than Manhattan, I learned, stretching nearly eighteen miles along the coast of Georgia. Access is only by boat; a ferry departs from St. Marys to make the round trip

just a few times a day. Ginger and I spent the night in a rental nearby and boarded the 9:00 a.m. ferry while still drinking our coffee.

For our first day we'd booked a Jeep tour of the island, a ride the website described as rugged. Our guide, Mike, met us at the dock, and straightway we were bumping along a primitive road to the north end of the island. We'd barely set out when we saw our first wild horse—a copper flash across a green field. Mike shared his binoculars so we could get a better look. I hoped it would be the first of many sightings.

Our Jeep rumbled past bristling palmetto stands as we listened to Mike build the layered tale of Cumberland's human history, a parade of native Guales and Timucuans of centuries ago, General Nathaniel Greene of Revolutionary War fame, and the fabulously wealthy Carnegies, who built a small village of mansions for their sprawling clan in the late 1800s. My notion of wild Cumberland quietly faded to accommodate this panoply of humanity.

At the Settlement, we explored the remains of a rustic village. More than three hundred people once lived there, and most were employed to run the Carnegie estate at the height of the family's residence. The diminutive First African Baptist Church sits nearby, the site of the secret wedding of John F. Kennedy Jr. and Carolyn Bessette. Paparazzi swarmed here afterward for photos and scraps of gossip when they found, to their horror, they had missed the event.

As we traveled the road south, Cumberland's wild creatures reasserted themselves. An alligator with a swollen belly lay motionless in a mud flat, his smile still and alien to our mammalian ways. Farther along, a male turkey strutted across the road, his dark tail raised against the spiky fans of saw palmetto.

We emerged from the tangle of forest in a clearing where we encountered the shining white apparition of Plum Orchard, the mansion of twenty-four thousand square feet of Greek Revival columns and Palladian arched windows built by Lucy Carnegie, the family matriarch, for her son George.

OPPOSITE: *Drapes of gray moss catch the sunlight in the trees above Nightingale Trail on Cumberland Island, creating the startling effect of a gauzy curtain over the green palmettos. I let the white of the paper flow from the trail upward through the trees, inviting the viewer to travel through this scene as we did: through the palmettos into a curtain of light.*

OPPOSITE: *Cumberland's bare and lonely beach called me to respond with meditative simplicity: a palette of only blue and earth tones, quiet support for the forms of the pines, stark against the sky and sand.*

At the front of the house stood a rough-skinned giant, a live oak of immense girth as wide as a room. Mike said it was five hundred years old, whereas some claim it is even older, perhaps six to eight hundred years. Ginger and I got out of the Jeep to embrace a segment of trunk and marvel. Each immense branch was as big as a tree, colonized with a veritable forest of ferns growing directly on the bark. This was resurrection fern, named for its miraculous ability to come back to life, green and growing, after seemingly drying up and dying during a drought.

Our tour ended at the burned ruins of Dungeness, the mansion built in the 1880s by the steel baron Tom Carnegie, brother of the more famous Andrew. Only the bones of the house remained, crumbling walls with bare chimneys soaring into the sky. But it was here that Tom's widow, Lucy, ruled the Carnegie estate after his death in 1886 and built a virtual fiefdom on the island. Mike painted a picture of the family's immense wealth and the vast grounds with more than forty outbuildings, spinning the tale until a veil of light and music, jewels and crystal, blurred the outlines of the ruin with a shimmering vision of the past.

Ginger and I returned the next day. We wanted to explore without the constraints of a tour. We wandered through the dreamy moss drapes of the maritime forest on Nightingale Trail. We crossed to the beach and sat on a bare driftwood tree. Tall, slender pines stood single file along the dunes, their limbs touching the sky. We looked up and down the wild and beautiful beach a final time in the hope of seeing a wild horse, but none appeared.

My picture of Cumberland, a remote barrier island, was swept aside for something new: an island big enough for both wilderness and the tides of human history.

—A. L.

The ruins of Dungeness.

After serving nine years as the superintendent of Yellowstone National Park, the first woman ever to hold that position, Suzanne Lewis retired in 2010 after an amazing thirty-two-year career with the National Park Service. Before that, she also had been the first woman superintendent at Glacier National Park and, before that, the Chattahoochee River National Recreation Area in Georgia. She also served as the first superintendent for the Park Service's Timucuan Ecological and Historical Preserve in Jacksonville, Florida, and the top manager of parks in the U.S. Virgin Islands.

But during all those years, another place, Cumberland Island National Seashore in coastal Georgia, was near and dear to her heart. Even though she lived in, and was the chief custodian of, some of America's most prized crown jewels, she said that Cumberland's serenity and solitude are unmatched.

And so she wants the island to be her final resting place. "It's in my will: When I die, I want my ashes strewn in the marshes of Cumberland," she said. While she loves all of the island, she said that the salt marsh is her favorite part: "The marsh is so peaceful and yet it teems with life." Cumberland, she added, still tugs at her heart as strongly as ever: "Cumberland Island has the greatest abundance of riches that I have ever encountered. The collection of riches in one place is unique, a word used too often and many times inaccurately but not when it comes to Cumberland. These riches are both immediate and subtle, from the sights and smells of the marshlands, forests, ocean, and ruins to the sounds that call to you once you are on the island. These sounds represent the voices of both the natural and cultural riches found on the island. From the first time I visited the island in 1979, I have felt that calling. Now . . . I look forward to hearing those welcoming voices, calling me back, time and time again."

For someone of Suzanne Lewis's remarkable background, that is an extraordinary testament to the magnificent splendor of Cumberland Island.

Legions of other visitors report coming away with similar feelings after visiting Cumberland. Larger than Manhattan, Cumberland is nearly three miles wide at its widest—the largest and southernmost barrier island of Georgia's famed coastal islands. Congress made the island a national seashore (a unit of the National Park Service) in 1972 and a few years later designated more than ninety-eight hundred acres of the island as a wilderness area.

The word *seashore* may not do Cumberland justice. It is, in fact, a complex ecological system of interdependent animal and plant communities. Wide sandy beaches and impressive dune systems protect the island from the sea. The island, in turn, protects the great salt marshes that separate the island from the mainland. Cumberland's interior is an intact maritime forest punctuated with freshwater ponds, saltwater coves, and swamps.

"These critical habitats harbor a wide diversity of life," says the Nature Conservancy. Loggerhead sea turtles nest on the island's northern beach, alligators inhabit the ponds and swamps, and large water birds like pelicans, egrets, and herons forage in the wetlands. Neotropical songbirds use the island as an important rest-and-refueling stop during their arduous migrations.

Ironically, the island's best-known creatures are not native. They are the feral horses that roam the island unfettered and at will. Many visitors come especially to see the so-called wild horses. The National Park Service's website for the island says, "A few horses were probably brought to Cumberland as livestock when Spanish missions were established in the late 1500s although evidence is scarce. The earliest historic account of horses on Cumberland Island was in 1742. During the battle between the Spanish and the English . . . [at] the north end of [the island], the Spanish found 'fifty to sixty horses in a corral within [Fort St. Andrews].'"

The island, however, was not always the natural sanctuary that it is now. During the era of King Cotton, before the Civil War, enslaved Africans cleared huge tracts of the island to grow the lucrative fiber. After the war, the island's new owners opted to let most of the island return to its natural state and maintain it that way.

Before the National Park Service acquired most of the island, nearly 90 percent of it was the private domain of Lucy and Thomas Carnegie and their descendants. (Thomas's brother Andrew amassed one of the world's greatest fortunes through iron and steel production.) Lucy and Tom Carnegie bought the island in the 1880s and built five mansions on it during the next two decades. The most superb house was the opulent fifty-nine-room Queen Anne–style Dungeness on the island's south end.

Dungeness burned nearly to the ground in 1959—arson was suspected—and today its ruins are a must-see for visitors.

But centuries before the Carnegies came to Cumberland, the island was host to a long succession of historic figures. Timucuan Indians inhabited the island before Europeans. Then came the Spanish, who successfully fought the French for possession of the island. Spanish Franciscan monks established two missions on the island to convert the Indians to Christianity. British soldiers then subdued the Spanish, setting the stage for white slaveowners to establish sprawling plantations on the island. About five hundred enslaved Africans toiled on the plantations to raise cotton for their white masters. After the Civil War, with King Cotton dethroned, Gilded Age industrialists, who thought it fashionable to own an island on the Georgia coast, assumed ownership of the island.

In 1972 Cumberland became the great national park that it is today, its natural beauty and richness protected and open to all for generations to come.

—C. S.

4 Ossabaw Island

Unspoiled barrier isle, a nesting site for the loggerhead turtle

I gripped the thin handrail of the boat as it crested another wave. We were entering Hell Gate, a narrow sea passage on the way from Savannah to our destination. At the wheel, the captain seemed unconcerned that six middle-aged women were perched precariously on the gunwales of his bouncing boat.

We were headed for one of Georgia's wildest places—Ossabaw Island.

It was Turtle Weekend, a trip organized by the Ossabaw Island Foundation, which manages Ossabaw in partnership with Georgia's Department of Natural Resources. This was our chance to learn about Georgia's sea turtles—and perhaps see a turtle nest hatching.

John "Crawfish" Crawford, a naturalist, sat at the bow of the boat and wasted no time in launching our education. His curly gray head seemed overflowing with a lifetime of lore about Georgia's salt marshes and the ways of their birds and wild creatures. In a tumble of words, he spilled the trove of his knowledge as we traveled through the waves.

Ossabaw, which is just south of Savannah, sparkled bright green on the horizon. I was unprepared for the shore's utter wildness: it could have been the New World a half-millennium ago. Welcoming us ashore was Elizabeth DuBose, the foundation's executive director, who showed us to our

OPPOSITE: *The travel sketches of Edward Lear, rendered in ink and watercolor, were the initial inspiration for my paintings when I began the Georgia natural wonders project. Lear rendered the structure and detail of a scene in ink and finished with broad washes of watercolor for hue and atmosphere. Here a sweep of dark blue in the foreground establishes the viewer's position in the shadows, while golden tints on the opposite shore show the warm early morning light on Ossabaw Island.*

Sicilian donkeys, introduced in 1965 by the island's then-owner, Eleanor "Sandy" Torrey West, roam the island.

accommodations. The century-old Club House, a restored 1880s hunting lodge, was tucked into the trees; it was built long before the island was designated a State Heritage Preserve in 1978.

After dinner, Crawfish gathered us around a table in the common room. There we found an array of turtle skulls, the dried shell of a green turtle, and a preserved turtle hatchling in a jar, which we inspected as Crawfish related the ecology of the island and the history of ongoing sea turtle conservation and research. Two solitary research residents had lived here all summer, he said, monitoring the turtle nests, counting hatchlings as they emerged. It appeared that fifty years of statewide conservation programs had been successful: a decade earlier, Georgia's annual count of sea turtle nests numbered 1,005. Now, in 2019, the count was 3,956. But Crawfish cautioned us: Hurricane Dorian had wreaked havoc that summer. The rising storm waters had drowned many eggs. He was preparing us for the nest we would see the next day.

The next morning I wandered outside with my mug of coffee to watch the sunrise over the marsh. The full moon was setting, faintly illuminating the ghostly forms of tall birds fishing in the water—wood storks and white egrets, large and small.

For this scene, I allowed washes of color to move and merge across the paper, creating the magic glow of moonlight and sunrise dissolving together. Fine pen-and-ink lines create the forms of the palms on the shore.

A Jeep appeared promptly after breakfast to take us to our destination for the day—South Beach—to see a turtle nest, a hatching, or whatever we might find.

The beach was a graveyard of trees, their twisted forms looming out of the sand like the bones of huge skeletons. We met the researchers, Brianna and Caleigh, at the nest site they had marked for the day's excavation. It had been sixty-five days since the mother loggerhead had laboriously dragged herself out of the sea to lay her eggs, leaving her trail in the sand. Caleigh began to dig. This was the reason we had come—to see the hatchlings.

But, as feared, there would not be a hatching. Caleigh brought the eggs out of the hole one by one—round, the size of Ping-Pong balls. All had drowned. She broke open one of the soft, permeable eggs to show us the unborn turtle with his tiny flippers.

Brianna reminded us of the good news, that turtles had laid more nests in Georgia that year than ever before. Many hatchlings were already safely in the ocean. More would hatch, no doubt.

On the return ride to the Club House, we were a quiet group. The ruined nest, though not unexpected, had dampened our spirits. Halfway back to the Club House we passed a leafless tree marking the edge of the marsh. Amid the branches we caught a glimpse of movement—a flash of bright pink.

There, strutting and bowing on the branches, were strange birds—roseate spoonbills! Prehistoric, with platypus-like beaks and bright red eyes, looking for all the world like the distant dinosaur cousins that they were. They cavorted like pink-plumed clowns, dipping and flapping their wings.

We watched for long minutes, this bright gift from a wild place.

Not what we had come for. But beautiful and rare just the same.

—A. L.

Ossabaw's rich salt marshes and tidal creeks support important migratory and wading birds, including this roseate spoonbill. To emphasize the astounding pink of his plumage, I used a simple complementary palette of rich green, allowing the background of the paper to create the bird's form and highlights.

In the mid-1970s, the growing tax burden was forcing the West and Torrey families to sell their beloved Ossabaw Island, one of the most pristine barrier islands on Georgia's coast. They fervently hoped that a conservation-minded individual or group would step up and buy the twenty-six-thousand-acre island paradise instead of letting it fall into the hands of developers who might turn it into another Hilton Head.

The State of Georgia, realizing that it had a rare opportunity to protect an unsullied coastal gem, became the island's salvation. In 1978, the state bought the island at just under half its appraised value, taking the generous offer of Eleanor "Sandy" Torrey West, who represented the families. For the bargain basement price of $8 million, in 1978 Georgia became the new owner and steward of Ossabaw, assuring that it would be left as a natural sanctuary for generations to come.

As part of the deal, the state consented to several stipulations at Sandy Torrey West's request. One was that she retain exclusive, lifetime use of a twenty-three-acre estate on the north end of the island, including her pink, stuccoed Spanish revival–style mansion. (She died in 2021 at age 108.)

Most important for Georgia was another stipulation: that Ossabaw become the state's first-ever natural heritage preserve, a designation that would bestow the highest level of state protection for the island. Accordingly, shortly after the Ossabaw purchase was finalized, Governor George Busbee issued an executive order "to protect, conserve, and preserve the natural and cultural resources of this Island for the benefit of present and future generations, and that Ossabaw Island shall only be used for natural, scientific, and cultural study, research, and education, and environmentally sound preservation, conservation, and management of the Island's ecosystem."

Today, Ossabaw Island is a precious, sparkling gem among Georgia's famous fourteen barrier islands. Its official caretaker is the Georgia Department of Natural Resources (DNR) in partnership with the Ossabaw Island Foundation.

Located twenty miles south of Savannah, Ossabaw is shaped like a wishbone with a splendid tidal marsh filling the middle. Roughly ten miles long and seven miles wide at its widest point, the island encompasses nearly nine thousand acres of high ground and seventeen thousand acres of marsh laced with twisting tidal creeks—the third largest island on Georgia's coast.

It is bordered by the white surf of the rolling Atlantic Ocean to the east; the Bear River of the Intracoastal Waterway to the west; the Ogeechee River to the north; and St. Catherines Sound to the south.

With its sandy white beaches, serene maritime forests, windswept sand dunes, freshwater ponds, and productive salt marshes, Ossabaw is typical of Georgia's barrier islands. Setting it apart, however, is its being left alone to flourish as nature intended. As such, its superb natural beauty and abundant ecosystems now inspire artists, scientists, and tree huggers alike.

Its more than ten miles of unblemished beaches are refuges for nesting loggerhead sea turtles and least terns, both endangered species. The "boneyard" beach on its south end, where encroaching ocean waters have turned massive pines, oaks, and cedars into sun-bleached skeletons, is an awe-inspiring sight. On the north end, sand dunes thirty feet high also are breathtaking.

Massive live oaks and several species of holly, southern magnolia, dogwood, and other hardwoods—all draped in Spanish moss—dominate the island's maritime forests. Towering cabbage palms (one of the few species of palm native to the Southeast), along with dense thickets of sawtooth palmetto, give the island a semitropical aura.

Its freshwater ponds are havens for bellowing alligators, frogs, small fish, wading birds, and migrating ducks and other waterfowl. Some ponds support noisy rookeries where herons, egrets, and other birds roost and raise their young.

The island's sweeping, mesmerizing salt marshes, dominated by vast stretches of cane-like smooth cordgrass (*Spartina alterniflora*), are some of the most productive ecosystems on Earth, nurseries for shrimp, blue crab, and other species of finfish and shellfish.

None of this is to say, however, that Ossabaw was never altered by human hands. Far from it. Like most of the other barrier islands, Ossabaw has a history of human occupation that goes back thousands of years.

Ossabaw was home to Native Americans for four thousand years before Europeans arrived in the sixteenth century. John Morel, a planter, began indigo cultivation and timbering in the 1760s. Various Morel descendants owned four separate tracts late in the nineteenth century. During Reconstruction (1865–1877), the Freedmen's Bureau controlled the island and awarded tracts on it to some formerly enslaved people. Dr. Henry Torrey and Nell Ford Torrey of Michigan bought the island in 1924. Their daughter was Sandy Torrey West.

During the island's plantation era in the eighteenth and nineteenth centuries, landowners cleared virgin forests for timber; for growing Sea Island cotton, rice, and indigo; and for raising free-range cattle, horses, hogs, and donkeys. Descendants of some of those animals, including hogs and donkeys, still roam the island unfettered. The feral hogs have evolved into a special breed famously known as Ossabaw pigs. They do much ecological harm but efforts to eliminate them—or at least substantially reduce their numbers—have been only moderately successful.

Even so, under the management of the DNR and the Ossabaw Island Foundation, the island's natural communities are quickly recovering from the impacts of humans. Because of Ossabaw's status as a heritage preserve, the number of visitors and various human activities are strictly limited.

The state's initial investment in Ossabaw has reaped untold dividends. It has made—and is still making—Ossabaw a living, robust example of what a lush barrier island, rich in natural splendor and biological diversity, was like before Europeans ever set foot in coastal Georgia.

—C. S.

5 Sapelo Island and Cabretta Beach

Marine sanctuary and Gullah-Geechee refuge

We were running late for the ferry. Sapelo Island in coastal McIntosh County is reachable only by water—no bridge or causeway crosses the wide marsh that separates it from the mainland. My friend Yasmin and I arrived with only a minute to spare. We climbed the ferry stairs to the top, where the breeze could keep us company for the crossing.

The boat launched into Doboy Sound. Immediately, a score of gulls took flight behind us, staging an aerial acrobatics show for the voyage. Their plumage varied: some hooded in black, others with gray eye patches, a few in pure white. Flying in our wake, the troupe swooped and dived behind us, each bird pirouetting and wheeling off in turn, as if to give each of its companions a turn in the spotlight.

We glided into Sapelo, where we were greeted by a big man. He introduced himself as J. R. Grovner, our guide for the day. The tour website had described him as a lifelong native of the island and a direct descendant of the West Africans captured and brought to the United States to work the plantations of the early 1800s. When J. R. and I spoke before the trip, he had assured me he could manage a special visit to Cabretta Beach, my destination. He would work it into the tour.

Yasmin and I boarded an old school bus with the other tour passengers. The bus lumbered along the meandering roads as J. R. shared, through a gravelly intercom, various morsels of Sapelo's human history from the time of prehistoric natives through the wealthy landowners of more recent years.

He stopped the bus several times to let us inspect points of interest—old tabby ruins, fading gravestones in a slave cemetery, and Reynolds Mansion, where industrialists wined and dined two U.S. presidents. J.R. said the mansion's last private owner, the tobacco heir R. J. Reynolds Jr., had planned to develop the island and promised to provide the African American landholders who lived on the island with electricity and running water—if they agreed to move and resettle in a central location, Hog Hammock, a small village already inhabited by some island families.

Reynolds's development plans never came to fruition, but the unintended result of his efforts was something unique: an isolated community of African Americans who had long preserved the Gullah-Geechee speech and crafts of their African forebears. Among these was the weaving of fish nets and sweetgrass baskets, created by hand much as they were by the enslaved people who arrived two centuries ago.

The bus rumbled into Hog Hammock. We stopped by a cluster of small, slightly ramshackle structures. COUNTRY STORE read the sign for the tiny general store, where tourists would customarily enjoy a cold Coke. It was closed now because of COVID. J. R. remarked that making a living on the island was difficult. The nearby marine institute once employed Hog Hammock locals, he said, "but not anymore. They're tryin' to get us to leave."

Somberly, we rode on, past live oaks, gray-haired giants hoary with thick Spanish moss. Palmettos fanned in dense crowds beneath them. Wildness was overtaking Sapelo and its dwindling human community.

J. R. stopped so we could photograph an alligator at the side of the road.

J. R. Grovner.

OPPOSITE: *The skeleton of the great live oak rises out of the sand, dark arms flailing like some giant sea creature struggling to escape a land-locked grave. Some of the tree limbs are rendered in line, others shaded, inviting the eye to dance between the flat plane of the paper and the illusion of sky and space.*

Then our guide turned the bus south—a detour, he explained, to "take a couple folks to Cabretta Beach." He meant Yasmin and me! We were about to see the wonder I had come for—what Charlie's list had named "one of the Atlantic coast's most beautiful undeveloped beaches." J. R. pulled over and pointed down a sandy road. "The beach is right over there." Eagerly, Yasmin and I got out. The other passengers peered at us curiously as the bus continued on its way to Sapelo's north end.

We were alone on a deserted road on an island cut off from the mainland. Yasmin and I looked at each other. J. R. had said he would return in ninety minutes.

We headed toward the shimmer of light at the end of the road. We stepped into a glittering world of white and blue, an endless stretch of sand and sea.

No scrap of plastic or trash marred the aching whiteness. Yasmin and I walked, sandpipers scattering ahead of us while stabbing at tiny shrimp-like creatures in the shallows. We stooped here and there to touch a few broken pieces of sand dollar, a satin fork of driftwood.

A lone tree, its beautiful skeleton scoured by wind and water, lay resting on the sand. Barnacles marched up its branches in bleached white rows. I sat down to draw. This is my favorite time in any nature trip—the moments I settle down to sketch in the quiet and see something new. I lost myself in the forms of the barnacles, tracing in ink the cones of delicate white plates overlapping like fragile sheets of armor.

Yasmin sat companionably close by. She broke open two water bottles to help us ward off the warm spring sun.

In the end it was R. J. Reynolds Jr. who helped create this island sanctuary, saving a wilderness for posterity. He founded the University of Georgia Marine Institute on Sapelo Island, bringing scientists from all over the world to study the salt marsh and its irreplaceable role in the ecology of the coast. So mixed with the undeniable ravages of human history was also some good.

Our time was almost over. Yasmin and I walked back to the pickup point. We passed a young man on the bank of a creek who was taking water samples. One of the Marine Institute's employees, no doubt.

We boarded the bus and returned on the ferry with the rest of the group. At the visitors center, a shelf of baskets caught my eye—sweetgrass. I picked up the one I liked best. On the back was written, in marker, "Yvonne Grovner." This was J. R.'s mom. The shop manager said weaving a basket of that size takes eight to ten hours. I did a quick mental calculation. The remuneration did not match the tiny stitches and exquisite artistry.

The basket now sits on my bookshelf at home, holding a sand dollar and a small twist of driftwood. It is a piece of enduring beauty, created somehow amid the sometimes ugly vagaries of our human story.

An astonishing miracle, like Sapelo Island itself.

—A. L.

A sketch from Sapelo Island.

Among marine scientists worldwide, Sapelo Island is sacred. Sapelo's global impact on marine biology can hardly be overstated. The undeveloped island is where legions of dedicated researchers, beginning in the 1950s, unraveled the mysteries of salt marshes and revealed the wetlands' vast importance for marine life and for humans as well.

Today, visitors can come to Sapelo to see where this groundbreaking research took place—and is still taking place. At the same time, they can take in the stunning natural beauty and serenity of Sapelo, one of the East Coast's most remote barrier islands, one that is surrounded by broad estuaries and sweeping salt marshes interlaced with twisting tidal creeks.

As if that were not enough to lure a visitor, Sapelo is also connected to two of the Atlantic coast's most scenic—yet totally undisturbed—beaches, Nanny Goat Beach and Cabretta Beach. Ecologists laud the wide sandy beaches as prime examples of barrier island environments that have never been developed—and therefore do their job as barriers.

Sapelo lies midway on the Georgia coast, in the center of the state's well-defined chain of barrier islands. The 16,500-acre island is Georgia's fourth largest and, except for the 434-acre African American community of Hog Hammock, is entirely owned and managed by the State of Georgia.

Sapelo's isolation and amazingly pristine environment—and R. J. Reynolds Jr.'s general backing—are what first drew scientists there in the early 1950s. They would conduct pioneering research on the ecology of salt marshes, estuaries, beaches, maritime forests, and other coastal ecosystems. Their work was made possible through the great generosity of Reynolds, a tobacco company heir who once owned Sapelo. Reynolds and the scientists together were largely responsible for establishing the University of Georgia Marine Institute on Sapelo's south end, providing the intrepid researchers with crucial support to conduct their field investigations.

Before the research on Sapelo, millions of acres of salt marsh around the world were regarded as little more than wastelands to be dredged, drained, filled in, and transformed into lucrative seaside real estate. But the Sapelo scientists, working in the unspoiled salt marshes around the island, learned otherwise.

They found that the marshes, estuaries, coastal ocean, and land interact as one great natural system. Impairment of one part of this magnificent system affects all others. The scientists were astounded when their research revealed the salt marsh's incredible productivity. Sapelo's marshes, they concluded, ranked with the most productive ecosystems on Earth. The organic material produced by the marshes, they discovered, fed an amazing array of fish and shellfish in the estuaries and coastal areas. Without the marshes, marine creatures great and small would starve to death. The marshes had other benefits: they protected the land from storms blowing in from the sea, and they cleansed polluted water. At the heart of this amazing system, the scientists learned, were the tides, whose ebbs and flows are crucial to stimulating marsh growth and maintaining coastal ecosystems.

The astonishing research helped convince even some of the most stubborn politicians to pass strict laws to protect all of Georgia's 368,000 acres of salt marsh and safeguard barrier island beaches and tidal creeks. Following Georgia's lead, other coastal states and nations around the world adopted their own seashore protection laws.

The impressive work on Sapelo caught the eye of the federal government. In December 1976, the National Oceanic and Atmospheric Administration (NOAA) designated 6,110 acres of the island as the Sapelo Island National Estuarine Research Reserve—the second such reserve in the nation at the time. NOAA called the new sanctuary a "Christmas present to the people of the nation." It included extensive tracts of pristine salt marsh, small islands within the marsh, maritime forest, a picturesque stretch of Nanny Goat Beach, and the entire Duplin River estuary on Sapelo's back side. The designation as a marine research reserve ensured that Sapelo would continue for many more years as an outdoor laboratory for important marine biology studies.

Through an agreement with NOAA, the Georgia Department of Natural Resources manages the reserve and conducts regular public tours of Sapelo. The tours start on the mainland at the reserve's visitors center—filled with informative exhibits and coastal artwork—in the community of Meridian, Georgia, near the town of Darien. From the dock there, visitors board a ferry to Sapelo, where they then hop on a bus for a sightseeing jaunt on the island. Among other things, the island tour includes a visit to the salt marsh, a walk on the unspoiled beach, views of a superb lighthouse, and a tour of the mansion formerly owned by Reynolds. The visitors center is also the place to arrange private tours and trips to Cabretta Beach.

No visit to Sapelo, however, would be complete without learning of the island's remarkable human history. Located on Sapelo is one of the most unusual archaeological features on Georgia's coast, a prehistoric ceremonial "shell ring" that attests to the presence of early Native Americans there. The name Sapelo is of Indian origin, later adapted as Zapala by the Spanish missionaries who established themselves on the island from about 1573 to 1686. In the 1840s, one of the most influential and innovative planters on Georgia's coast, Thomas Spalding, came to own most of Sapelo. He introduced the cultivation of sugar cane and the manufacturing of sugar in Georgia and built a sugar mill on Sapelo. He also raised Sea Island cotton. To work his antebellum plantation empire, Spalding and his children owned 385 enslaved people on Sapelo by the 1850s.

After the Civil War, some of the formerly enslaved workers managed to acquire some acreage on Sapelo. However, Spalding's descendants sold the vast majority of the island to Howard Coffin, a wealthy northern industrialist. Coffin later sold Sapelo to Reynolds, whose heirs sold the island to the State of Georgia. The sale did not include the enclave known as Hog Hammock, where several descendants of Spalding's enslaved laborers live today. Hog Hammock is the last intact Gullah-Geechee community on Georgia's coast. Its residents keep alive the culture and many of the traditions of their forebears, who were forcibly brought from their homes in Africa.

In essence, Sapelo's rich human history, pivotal scientific studies, and extraordinary natural beauty make it one of the most fascinating places you will find in Georgia.

—C. S.

6 Woody Pond, Harris Neck National Wildlife Refuge

Georgia's Wild Kingdom

The blue heron stalked the water's edge, seemingly oblivious to the six-foot alligator lying motionless just a few feet away.

My friend Yasmin and I watched from the trail, transfixed. Yasmin clutched my arm. "The alligator is going to get him!" She held out her hand. "Look—I'm shaking! I'm not kidding, I'm *deathly* afraid of alligators."

It was March, and we were at Woody Pond in Harris Neck National Wildlife Refuge, about thirty miles southwest of Savannah. It is home to one of the country's largest nesting sites for the endangered wood stork. In his bucket list column, Charlie Seabrook had written, "In spring, thousands of egrets, herons and endangered wood storks form spectacular nesting colonies." I had arrived in early spring because I did not want to risk missing the sight.

The heron took a step closer to the big reptile. At that instant, a flash of movement drew our eyes—something across the pond—the figure of a woman, approaching along the trail at the water's edge. "We need to warn her!" Yasmin said.

"I think alligators usually try to get *away* from people," I murmured, a reassurance as much for myself as for Yasmin.

The woman strolled closer to the heron, appearing to look at him and the reptile with interest. Emboldened, we joined her. She nodded at us. "The birds don't usually stand this close to the gators," she remarked.

Yasmin was still hanging back. "Aren't the alligators dangerous?"

She smiled. "Not usually. I've been walking here every day for ten years—the only time I've seen a gator get aggressive is if you're bothering them—or if you have a dog," she added, as an afterthought.

Her name was Virginia. We learned she lived near the back entrance to the park and volunteered regularly at the pond as a guide. Hearing that I was interested in the wood storks, she advised me to come back in May. She pointed to the trees on the islands in the middle of the pond. "The treetops will be white with all the birds nesting. It's really something."

Yasmin and I spent the day exploring the trails. A half-dozen ponds created in the 1960s harbor a virtual Wild Kingdom of wildlife. On one shoreline, we looked in amazement at scores of great white egrets, gathered like ghosts in the brush. Ibises and herons waded in the shallows, dipping long beaks into the water to feed.

But I was haunted by the description of "white trees" around the pond, and I plotted our return in two months. Yasmin agreed to return with me.

Thus, an early May morning found us back at Woody Pond. The morning sun was luminous, and its light revealed a scene that seemed straight from the Garden of Eden. Wild creatures inhabited every space: in the water, on the shore, and in the air. Across the pond, just as Virginia had described, the treetops were white with the feathers of nesting wood storks, and the air was filled with the cries of the hungry offspring. Flutters and flashes of wings set the treetops in motion as the parent storks came and went, feeding the clamoring nestlings.

OPPOSITE: *Water and shoreline at Woody Pond overflow with primordial wildlife. In this painting, watercolor in a range of hues moves freely across the paper to convey the liquid quality of the morning light, the drawn shapes of the animals dissolving into the sun.*

An immense bull alligator blended almost unseen into the shoreline. Here the shape of the reptile is sculpted with line over a swirl of color, so that he emerges from the surrounding vegetation as he appeared—part of the landscape itself.

Standing in the water before us, and perched on remains of tree stumps, were a multitude of shore birds: white egrets, herons, and the motionless anhinga, its outstretched wings flashing silver in the sun. In the shallows, baby alligators lay everywhere, piled like puppies on logs and in the mud. And in the deeper waters, we spied the big gators cruising, trailing glittering ripples behind them. A nearby sign explained that the deadly reptiles, although ready to make a meal of any juvenile fallen from the nest, offer an essential benefit: their constant patrol keeps other predators, such as raccoons and opossums, from snatching eggs and babies from the storks' shoreline nests. The thieves do not dare cross the water.

Suddenly the air was filled with a deep vibration, a sound that grew louder and deeper until it was a subterranean rumble, thrumming across the pond for many seconds. We looked around—what was going on?! An answering roar sounded across the pond. We looked on in awe as big bull alligators rose from the water to sound their territorial cries.

Woody Pond pulses with life—a piece of living Creation, where nature's wild creatures live on, abundant.

—A. L.

Great white egrets mass thickly along the shoreline, their shapes merging in an undulating pattern of white plumage and blue shadows. A few ink lines for feathers and twigs bring definition to the soft washes.

The Harris Neck National Wildlife Refuge is for the birds. Its nearly twenty-eight hundred acres encompass an array of habitats—salt marsh, freshwater ponds, open fields, swampland, mixed pine and hardwood forests—that support a remarkable diversity of bird species. Birders have spotted an amazing 342 species in the refuge. Of those, eighty-three species nest there in spring and summer in the various habitats.

Located in McIntosh County midway on Georgia's coast, the inland refuge is an important link for migratory and nesting birds in a chain of refuges stretching along the Atlantic seaboard. Because of its accessibility and bird diversity, Harris Neck is also one of the eighteen sites that form Georgia's Colonial Coast Birding Trail.

An annual avian spectacle draws most visitors to Harris Neck. Beginning in early March, several species of long-legged wading birds start forming a huge, spectacular rookery at Woody Pond, a fifty-acre engineered pool fed by well water, one of six such ponds in Harris Neck. The birds—egrets, ibises, herons, and others—congregate there by the thousands, side by side, to lay their eggs in big treetop nests of loose sticks and other material. By May, nearly every tree and shrub around the freshwater pond and on its small bushy islands are crowded—and cacophonous—with the birds tending nests filled with downy newly hatched chicks.

For one wading bird species, the wood stork, Woody Pond is more than just a nesting place: it helped rescue the majestic bird from the brink of extinction. The mostly white-plumaged creature is North America's only stork species. Standing about three feet tall, the lanky bald-headed bird feeds by wading with its long, opened beak partially submerged, snapping it shut when it touches a small fish or other prey. The stork often shuffles its feet and flashes its beautiful black-and-white wings to stir up potential prey, which it then captures. Though it looks gawky on land, the bird is a graceful flier with its neck and long legs stretched straight out.

During the 1980s, however, wildlife scientists feared that the wood stork would be extinct by 2000 because of its rapidly declining numbers. Many of the wetlands—mostly in Florida—where the bird nested and foraged had been ditched and drained for development, agriculture, and pine plantations. The bird was added to the federal list of endangered species in 1983. Unless the species made a remarkable recovery, it would sink into oblivion.

Then, in 1987, a remarkable thing happened: biologists were thrilled to find eighteen pairs of wood storks nesting in black gum trees around Woody Pond—the first time the birds had ever nested there. But a couple of years later, the biologists' elation nose-dived when a dry spell caused water levels to drop and allow raccoons to destroy most of the stork nests.

In response, the U.S. Fish and Wildlife Service pumped more water into Woody Pond to deepen it by six feet. That deterred the raccoons, which are leery of swimming through alligator-filled water, but the higher water levels also killed most of the black gum trees in which the storks nested. Biologists then came up with an ingenious solution—artificial nesting structures, basically platforms on poles, that would substitute for the trees that died. The storks eventually began building their nests on the tall structures. Meanwhile, the wildlife service planted in the pond dozens of cypress trees, which are more tolerant of standing water. As they grew, they created small islands, and by 2006 the platforms were no longer needed because the wood storks had begun nesting in the now-thriving cypresses.

This project, and other efforts elsewhere by state and federal wildlife managers, helped reverse the wood stork's plummeting numbers. In June 2014, Sally Jewel, then the interior secretary, came to Woody Pond to make an important announcement: the wood stork, she said, was being upgraded from endangered to threatened, an indication that it no longer faced extinction—another great success story of the Endangered Species Act.

Today, more than four hundred pairs of wood storks nest at Woody Pond, making it Georgia's largest inland wood stork rookery and one of the most important in the Southeast. The refuge is now an important link in the effort to bolster stork populations. Many of the stork babies reared there each spring—two to three per nest—disperse and help establish new breeding colonies elsewhere in the Southeast.

Harris Neck's managers now bill the wood stork as one of the refuge's two signature species. Its other signature species is the painted bunting, a sparrow-size bird that favors nesting habitat in the refuge's maritime scrub areas. The male painted bunting may be North America's most colorful songbird, with its striking blue head, red underparts, and yellow-green back—a fusion of neon-bright colors that seem to be right out of a child's coloring book.

But the wood stork and painted bunting represent only part of Harris Neck's diversity. Since its inception as a wildlife refuge in 1962, Harris Neck has become a premier nesting, foraging, and wintering habitat for scores of bird species and other wildlife.

During spring and fall migrations, other colorful songbirds—warblers, vireos, grosbeaks, flycatchers, thrushes, and the like—fill Harris Neck's woodlands, fields, and other habitats. Several duck species also find havens at Harris Neck: in winter, large concentrations of ducks, including teal, mallards, and gadwalls, gather in the freshwater ponds and marshlands. Occasionally, visitors spot roseate spoonbills foraging among other wading birds in the ponds.

Harris Neck, though, has not always been a wildlife haven. After the Civil War, formerly enslaved people who had worked the big plantations in the area became owners of dozens of small plots at Harris Neck. They formed a tight community and raised vegetables, cattle, chickens, and hogs; they fished in the tidal river and salt marsh creeks. But in 1942, when the United States entered World War II, the government chose Harris Neck as the site for an Army Air Force base from which flight personnel would hunt Nazi submarines lurking off the U.S. coast. Using its power of eminent domain, the federal government forced the African American farmers on Harris Neck to abandon their community. The landowners later claimed that the government had promised that they could buy their land back after the war, when the military base no longer was needed.

However, when the war ended, the government gave its Harris Neck property to McIntosh County. But after a series of scandals involving use of the property by some county officials, the federal government repossessed the land and in 1962 deeded it to the U.S. Fish and Wildlife Service to be managed as a national wildlife refuge.

Today, few signs of the military's former presence at Harris Neck remain—except for the old weed-covered concrete runways that once accommodated the submarine-hunting aircraft. However, among the descendants of Harris Neck's displaced former residents, resentment of the government has never faded. They demand that the land taken from their ancestors in the 1940s be returned to the heirs. The land in question constitutes about a fourth of the Harris Neck refuge.

The federal government has been adamant in its refusal to return the land to the descendants, saying that the original owners in 1942 were fairly compensated for giving up their farms. The descendants continue to press their case nonetheless.

Meanwhile, the wading birds come back year after year to hatch and raise new generations at Woody Pond. And the once-endangered wood stork continues to thrive there.

—C. S.

7 Ebenezer Creek

Cypress-gum swamp where thousand-year-old trees abide

Ebenezer Creek, twenty miles upriver from the city of Savannah, is home to thousand-year-old cypress trees. As I read this description from Charlie's list, the image of a gnarled and ancient tree flickers in my mind, like a memory from some time or place I can't quite recall.

I want to see an ancient tree.

It's late fall, and the sun sails in a clear sky over Ebenezer Creek in southeast Georgia. I steer my kayak into the slow-moving current, floating on a river that seems to have no banks as it flows far into the surrounding trees.

My guide, a pleasant young woman named Cassandra, paddles her kayak just ahead of me. She begins my education as soon as we leave the boat launch. "Ebenezer Creek is a State Scenic River—the only one on the coastal plain. It's a good example of the ecosystem called 'blackwater creek.' Ecologists say it's the best cypress-gum swamp still left in the Savannah River Basin." Cassandra's voice is animated, her love of this place clear. Paddling at leisurely intervals, she illuminates some peculiarities—how to tell the trunks of cypresses from tupelo gums, where to look for the high-water mark on the trees, and what kinds of wildlife are found in and around the water—a variety of wading birds, owls, alligators, and frogs, as well as more uncommon species, such as the silky camellia and prothonotary warbler.

OPPOSITE: *A trio of mighty cypresses rises from the blackwater creek, dark silhouettes against the dancing colors of the sunlit foliage behind. The small form of the kayaker at left on the Ebenezer Creek bank offers a clue to the size of the surrounding trees.*

She pauses, and we float into the silence, our kayaks skimming a shadowy underworld of reflections. I'm reminded of the Okefenokee. But Ebenezer Creek feels darker and older. Near the water, the trees swell into imposing bulk, eight or twelve feet wide. We pass hulking giants that trail great beards of silvery moss. Cassandra says that core measurements show some of Ebenezer's cypresses began their lives a millennium ago.

Perhaps we are looking at one.

Cassandra's narrative turns to Ebenezer's human story—the native Americans, then the Salzbergers, religious refugees who settled the area in the early 1700s. The latter helped shape the early laws of colonial Georgia, rejecting slavery and plantation agriculture; however, their settlement was destroyed in the Revolutionary War. During the Civil War, the creek was the site of the Ebenezer Creek Massacre. A historical marker near the creek tells the sad story:

> On December 9, 1864, during the American Civil War, U.S. Gen. Jeff. C. Davis crossed Ebenezer Creek (via pontoon bridges) with his 14th Army Corps as it advanced toward Savannah during Gen. William T. Sherman's March to the Sea. Davis [then] hastily removed the pontoon bridges over the creek, and hundreds of freed slaves following his army drowned trying to swim the swollen waters to escape the pursuing Confederates. Following a public outcry, Sec. of War Edwin Stanton met with Sherman and local black leaders in Savannah on January 12, 1865. Four days later, President Lincoln approved Sherman's Special Field Orders No. 15, confiscating over 400,000 acres of coastal property and redistributing it to former slaves in 40-acre tracts.

Hulking cypress trees loom in the shadows, somehow untouched by the fleeting moments of human history—flashes of folly and fury across the silent centuries.

We drift into the light. The sun has robed a trio of giant tupelo gums in gold. Again, I feel an elusive memory stir and then rise.

I see a day in my early adolescence, the summer after my thirteenth birthday, when I pause on that step between child and adult. In that golden season, my best friend and I steep ourselves in books, fantasies by Tolkien and C. S. Lewis. Joined by my sister Jane, my friend Tracy and I read constantly, immersing ourselves in faraway worlds. We memorize their maps, learn their languages, and lose ourselves in the stories, tarrying in the magic world of childhood, wanting not to leave.

We set out one afternoon to follow the small river that flows between our neighborhoods. We are eager to escape the tame world of our yards and houses. We want to walk the woods and travel in a land only we three can see. Hushed, excited, we create together, speaking aloud of the shadows we pass.

The oak tree looming on the bank is a dark presence silently watching us; the mossy sycamore biding its time permits us passage in a kingdom of green and growing things; an immense rock atop a cliff turns its stony profile toward us—every rock and every tree is alive, not entirely of this world.

Abruptly, I surface.

The memory fades, and my eyes focus on the scene before me. Cassandra and I have arrived at the end of the tour. It's late afternoon, and the sun burnishes every tree and leaf with gold. I take photo after photo of this luminous landscape—a glowing world of green and gold and orange. I think I have never seen a place so beautiful. My last glimpse of Ebenezer Creek is a cypress tree standing in the light, a tall, graceful form, raising her limbs in a farewell—or perhaps it is a blessing.

I am like a traveler returned from a distant journey. I remain in my memories, half in that other place, as I go to sleep that night—

Not leaving 'til the morning, when I wake in the plain daylight of the world.

—A. L.

OPPOSITE: *The late afternoon sun etches the graceful cypress and surrounding creek banks with light. I traced the lines of moss hanging in the trees with a watercolor brush, hairs splayed in a fan shape. Rendered in soft gray, the lines impart detail without distracting from the main event—the luminous reflections on the water.*

The bald cypress and the tupelo gum are the classic embodiments of southern swamps. Draped in Spanish moss and rising more than eighty feet from brownish-black swamp water, the trees cast a distinctive, mesmerizing beauty that makes so-called cypress-gum swamps the destinations of nature lovers.

Ebenezer Creek passes through one of Georgia's most outstanding examples of such a swamp. The creek, in fact, is the heart of the swamp. A blackwater tributary of the lower Savannah River, the thirteen-mile stream attracts visitors from all over the South. In canoes and kayaks, they paddle the waterway at an unhurried pace to view the watery forest of ancient cypresses and tupelo gums and its abundant wildlife.

Because of its haunting splendor and rich ecosystem, a seven-mile segment of Ebenezer Creek is one of only three rivers that Georgia has designated as part of the Georgia Scenic River System (not to be confused with the National Wild and Scenic River System; Georgia's Chattooga River is the state's only river in the latter) and the only such river on the coast. In 1976, the U.S. secretary of the interior accorded the creek another honor—the creek and 1,350 acres of its swamp became one of Georgia's eleven members of the National Natural Landmarks Program.

In particular, naturalists say that the bald cypresses, with their remarkably large buttresses, are what make Ebenezer Creek a strikingly scenic waterway. The huge buttresses, which give rise to arrow-straight trunks, are what many visitors come to see. Shaped like giant, inverted ice cream cones, the deeply ridged buttresses at the trees' bases may stretch eight to twelve feet wide. When reflected in the dark swamp water, they look like small islands. The late Charles Wharton (1923–2003), revered as one of Georgia's foremost naturalists, said he was at a loss for words when he tried to adequately describe "the gigantic buttresses of the cypresses of Ebenezer Creek." After he and other scientists carefully examined the cypresses, they concluded that several are, amazingly, more than one thousand years old, hundreds of years older than any other living trees in Georgia. The cypresses' high resistance to rot and their drought tolerance, Wharton suggested, contribute to their incredible longevity.

Cypress buttresses, scientists believe, may help support a tree in wet, unstable soil and aid in oxygen intake. But the appendages for which bald cypresses are really best known are their knobby knees, special kinds of roots that protrude upward from the water at the trees' feet. Some knees of Ebenezer Creek's cypresses may be taller than a person. The knees also may allow a tree to take in oxygen and provide additional support in the soggy soil. The truth is, though, no one really knows the function of cypress knees. One other characteristic sets bald cypresses apart: although they are conifers, they shed their needle-like leaves in the fall even though most conifers are evergreens. Their needle shedding is why they are called bald cypress.

Equally prominent in Ebenezer Creek's arboreal splendor are the long-lived tupelo gum trees (*Nyssa aquatica*). They are actually deciduous hardwoods, but they also thrive in the swamp water, often side by side with the bald cypresses. One of the most scenic portions of Ebenezer Creek lies near its mouth, where a forest of tupelo gums towers above the reflective, inky black water. Their regular pattern and soaring heights give the impression of a temple or a cathedral. The tupelos also have swollen bases, although not nearly as dramatic as those of bald cypresses'. Tupelo buttresses, however, have unusual counterclockwise twisting, but the cause is a scientific mystery. Typically, tupelos have long straight trunks; narrow open crowns of spreading branches; and large, deciduous, shiny leaves—though in a pure stand of tupelos, their trunks often are somewhat crooked above their swollen bases. One other thing that tupelo gums are known for: honeybees make a prized honey from tupelo flower nectar in spring.

Ebenezer Creek's unusual hydrology—or natural plumbing system—may, in large part, be responsible for its amazing natural environment and scenery. The creek is described as both a blackwater and a backwater stream. Blackwater streams are slow-moving waters flowing through forested swamps or wetlands. As vegetation decays, tannins leach into the water, lending a dark stain that resembles black tea to a transparent acidic water.

Ebenezer is also considered a backwater creek because its water levels rise—as much as eight feet—and fall in concert with flow levels in the Savannah

River. When the river rises during seasonal floods and heavy rains, its water backs up into the creek and swamp. The swamp's water may remain high for long periods and cause oxygen in the water to drop to low levels, which may be responsible for the bald cypresses' enormous buttresses. (Scientists believe the swollen buttresses provide inundated trees with an increased surface area for oxygen intake.) The backing up may have one other important impact—low levels of nutrients. A poor nutrient supply may be why Ebenezer's cypresses have trunks of unusually small diameters despite the old age and gigantic buttresses of the trees. That, however, might have been their salvation—loggers often did not bother with trees with small trunks.

—C. S.

8 The Altamaha

Georgia's Little Amazon

Alligators and six-foot-long sturgeon are said to swim in the depths of the murky water passing beneath our boat. My friend Ginger steered from the stern of the kayak as I alternately paddled and snapped photos. We were deep in South Georgia, navigating America's wildest unbroken stretch of river on the Atlantic seacoast: the Altamaha, which flows freely for 137 miles with no dam to break its course to the sea. It begins at the confluence of the Oconee and Ocmulgee Rivers, roughly east of Tifton and west of Statesboro, and empties into the Atlantic near Darien.

The river is known as Georgia's Little Amazon.

We had come for a weekend trip with the Georgia Conservancy to encounter the river as those who love it say it should be done: on the water. We joined seventy fellow enthusiasts from all over the Southeast, our bright boats and life vests forming a colorful parade gliding atop the water. On either side, the wide fingers of the Altamaha spread quietly between trunks of cypress and tupelo gums.

The silence was eerie. Small drips and splashes followed our paddles through the water—but no rumble of engine or motorboat disturbed the quiet.

The river inhaled a slow tidal breath from the sea. Our kayaks, dreamlike, seemed to stand still upon the water as miles of wild riverbank passed in a shimmer before our eyes, swamp trees and moss etched in light from the morning sun.

Clark, our leader and the longtime trips director for the conservancy, gave a voice to the river. The Altamaha, he said, drains fourteen thousand square miles of Georgia—the third largest watershed in the country. Depending on whom you ask, the river waters, its swamps and sand ridges, harbor 100–130 species of rare plants and animals. And yet, he said, this wilderness is so little known that the Altamaha is often called "the river that nobody knows."

As the afternoon wore on, swamp forest gave way to rustling marsh grass. Clark told us that when the spring rains come, the Altamaha becomes as much as five miles wide as it spreads across the floodplain at the coast. He scanned the sky and pointed to a bald eagle high in the blue swooping down to alight on a lone tree. The afternoon waned, and we drew near the town of Darien, our take-out point. We still had met no signs of human life. We heard no sound but the murmur of wind in the grass.

The wild Altamaha kept its ancient quiet.

The second day was another gift. We were to venture into the deep swamp creeks surrounding the campground—the "best part of the weekend," returning paddlers assured us. We set out at midmorning. One kayak after another, we threaded our way through the trees, time travelers in an ancient forest of water that once stretched across the coastal South.

Trunks of cypress and tupelo loomed in every direction. The Altamaha threw its watery chains among them as though to claim the bottomland entirely. Trees wavered in endless mirrored reflections.

We were a full hour into the swamp when Ginger and I noticed the water, a cold sloshing over our seats. A leak! The kayak had already taken in a few

OPPOSITE: *To float down the Altamaha is to follow a column of light as it opens over the river, connecting water to sky. This painting shows the moss-draped trees and the distant forms of the kayakers dissolving together into that liquid pour of light.*

A four-legged stowaway—a Pekingese smuggled into the kayak group by his owner—enjoys the paddle into Darien.

inches. We looked around.

Trees crowded close, but no land was in sight.

I remembered now the warning in boldface on our registration form: "Intermediate Paddlers Only." I had figured that was only code for "I've been in a kayak before."

Clark pulled up behind us. "This is where it gets a little tough for a tandem kayak," he said with empathy. "Y'all have much experience?"

No.

Experience would have been handy, because steering a leaky twelve-foot kayak out of a thicket of trees is no simple chore.

We weren't the only ones struggling. Kayaks began to pile up like bumper cars among the trees. One was stuck fast between fallen cypress trunks, another filled with water, threatening to capsize. Our group had become a floating traffic jam. For a few tense minutes, I forgot all about enjoying the Altamaha wilderness—I wanted only to get out of the swamp without taking a swim.

However, with some maneuvering and a bit of assistance from Clark, our group was finally untangled. We resumed our zigzag course among the trees and made it to the end of an afternoon full of magic and wonder. Ginger and I arrived back at camp with the others with only a little bailing along the way. I was even hopeful that by now I was, indeed, an intermediate paddler.

That night, once again, we gathered around the campfire, sharing favorite memories of the weekend. As we left the fireside for our tent, the call of the barred owl came clearly from the swamp. Ghostly plumes of pale indigo glimmered along the riverbanks. The stars sang brightly in the velvet black, as they have since the beginning of the world.

And at dawn we awakened to see a great white egret silently stalk the shoreline in the mist.

I was privileged to witness a true wilderness remaining in Georgia—and to meet the river that nobody knows.

—A. L.

The great white egret appeared in the mist at sunrise, silently stalking the river's edge. Delicate lines of blue ink define all but the bird itself, with a tangle of vines outlining the negative space of the egret's graceful silhouette. In this way, the painting re-creates what we experienced that morning—the slow revelation of the egret in the mist.

The Altamaha is neither the longest nor the best-known river in Georgia. But it is the mightiest. Together, the Altamaha and its tributaries drain all or part of fifty-three Georgia counties, one fourth of the entire state. So much freshwater comes down the Altamaha that some liken it to the Nile. During a year of normal rainfall, the river pumps more than three trillion gallons of freshwater—100,000 gallons per second—into the Atlantic Ocean, one-sixth of the southeast coast's entire freshwater output.

If the Altamaha's massive outflow makes it mighty, its superb beauty and ecological importance make it magnificent—one of the most important natural jewels in the eastern United States. Conservationists call it "the perfect image of a true southern river" as it meanders through rich bottomland hardwood swamps, cypress-tupelo sloughs, oxbow lakes, former rice fields, sweeping salt marshes, a broad multichannel delta, and finally into a biologically rich estuary occupying much of Glynn and McIntosh Counties. Because of the Altamaha's unique character and sheer biodiversity, the Nature Conservancy, a world-renowned conservation group, named the river one of the Last Great Places and established the Altamaha River Bioreserve in 1991.

The river, its tributaries, and associated habitats support the largest concentration of rare species of any river system in Georgia. Its wide delta, woods, swamps, marshes, and saltwater estuary are refuges for well more than one hundred species of rare or endangered plants and animals—such as West Indian manatees, piping plovers, eastern indigo snakes, gopher tortoises, eleven species of mussels, the hairy rattleweed, swallowtail kites, and others.

Migratory fish such as American shad, herring, and the endangered shortnose sturgeon spawn in the river. Just offshore, the river pumps nutrients and freshwater into the ocean that help sustain a vibrant shrimp population, the basis of a commercial fishery valued at $20 million a year. Farther out to sea, nearly eighteen miles due east of Sapelo Island, the river's outflow helps support an underwater subtropical paradise—Gray's Reef National Marine Sanctuary.

The Altamaha's headwaters rise about 250 miles from the sea, near the bustling cities of Atlanta and Athens in the red clay hills of Georgia's northern Piedmont region. The headwaters merge and form the Altamaha's two main tributaries, the Ocmulgee and the Oconee, major rivers in their own right. They form the Altamaha when they meet in Wheeler County in the heart of southern Georgia. The Altamaha then winds across the coastal plain, unfettered and unobstructed, to the sea, making it the largest intact, free-flowing river system on the East Coast.

Midway on the Georgia coast the river meets the sea in Altamaha Sound, a twenty-six-square-mile estuary. There, the river's freshwater blends with the ocean's saltwater to create one of the largest intact, high-quality estuaries—an angler's paradise—in the world. Lying at the outer edge of the estuary, at the mouth of the Altamaha, is the fifty-one-hundred-acre Wolf Island National Wildlife Refuge, a nursery for loggerheads and a sanctuary for at-risk, threatened, and endangered shorebirds and waterbirds. The refuge also includes Egg Island and Little Egg Island, breathtakingly beautiful places made up primarily of waving expanses of salt marsh with strips of sand and other coastal vegetation.

Upstream, vast bottomland hardwood swamps occupy the floodplains on each side of the river. Trees hundreds of years old live in the alligator-inhabited wetlands. When the swamps flood from heavy rains in winter and spring, about eighty species of fish—including several species of bass, sunfish, suckers, catfish, darters, carp, and minnows—may arrive to feed, reproduce, and seek refuge from predators. Just as important are the immense amounts of organic matter, such as decaying leaves and twigs, that the swamp sends into the river. Natural weathering and voracious microbes break much of it down into key nutrients and tiny bits and pieces of organic carbon that flow downstream and are trapped by the estuary and tidal marshes. The nutrients are natural fertilizers that nourish the salt marshes' signature plant, smooth cordgrass. The sediments that the river carries help build, maintain, and stabilize the marshes, two barrier islands (Sapelo and St. Simons), and the expansive river delta that is crucial winter feeding ground for thousands of migratory shorebirds.

The Altamaha's human history may be just as fascinating as its natural splendor. Timucuan Indians built towns and villages along the river. Crude dugout canoes, Spanish galleons, steamboats, and huge rafts of cut timber plied its lower stretches over the centuries. The river is associated with one of the world's greatest botanical legends—a mysterious flowering tree that the famed botanists John Bartram and his son William found in October 1765 on a sand ridge along the river's lower stretch. They named it the *Franklinia alatamaha* in honor of Benjamin Franklin and the river. When seeds collected by the Bartrams were grown in a garden, they produced a white, sweetly fragrant flower similar to the camellia. But nearly forty years later, the beautiful *Franklinia* had vanished from the lower Altamaha and has not been seen in the wild since (according to the North Carolina State Extension Service, it is notoriously difficult to grow).

Before the Civil War, the Altamaha Delta, where the river splits into four channels, was home to several historic rice and cotton plantations, most notably Hofwyl and Butler, where enslaved people toiled long hours in the fields. In particular, Butler Plantation became notorious for the harsh treatment of the enslaved laborers by its white managers. Fanny Kemble Butler, who was married to the plantation's owner, Pierce Butler, exposed the overseers' cruelty in 1863 in her powerful abolitionist book, *Journal of a Residence on a Georgian Plantation*.

The Altamaha was a legendary transportation route for the Georgia timber trade through the nineteenth century, when scores of huge timber rafts were lashed together to deliver logs to the ports of Brunswick and Darien. Much of the timber was virgin longleaf pine cut from along the Altamaha. Darien became the greatest lumber port in eastern America, where the timber was loaded onto timber schooners and transported to international markets such as Liverpool and Havana.

The Altamaha has one other distinction that sets it apart from most other rivers in the Southeast—it's one of the most protected waterways in the region. Since 1968, state and federal agencies (including the military), conservation groups, and others have been acquiring huge chunks of land, piece by piece, along the river. Today, both sides of the lower Altamaha are legally protected in a forty-two-mile unbroken corridor that begins near the town of Ludowici and ends at the Wolf Island refuge on the coast. In theory, a person could travel the length of the Lower Altamaha and never leave protected land. That includes the twenty-seven-thousand-acre Altamaha Wildlife Management Area with riverside trails for visitors; the Altamaha River Waterfowl Management Area, which encompasses the old Butler Island Plantation; the Lewis Island Natural Area (reached only by boat) containing a remarkable virgin cypress tidewater forest with Georgia's oldest trees; and many other tracts teeming with nature's wonders.

—C. S.

9 Broxton Rocks

Rugged rock formation holds rare matrix of plants and animals deep in South Georgia

"You see the way the leaf curls up? This is blackjack oak. It's different from the flat leaves on a white oak—that [the blackjack's] curl is a fire adaptation. It helps the leaf catch fire more easily. All this area was originally longleaf pine savannah—fire is part of the ecology."

Frankie Snow spoke with intense focus. I was seeing Broxton Rocks Preserve with a man whom Charlie Seabrook had called "one of the foremost naturalists in the state of Georgia." Joining Frankie was Jim Cottingham, who introduced himself as a fellow enthusiast eager for any opportunity to learn from Frankie and seemed to take the role of gracious host for this personal tour. Later I learned that Jim is a retired vice president of South Georgia State College, where Frankie is a professor emeritus.

I didn't know much about Broxton Rocks in rural Coffee County, but I was eager to learn—prepared for wonders.

Broxton Rocks is a four-mile-long glimpse into the subterranean layer of the coastal plain in the southeast quadrant of the state. Here the waters of Rocky Creek have carved an opening through the plain's shallow soils to reveal the Altamaha Formation, a band of sandstone that lies beneath fifteen thousand square miles of the coastal plain. At Broxton Rocks the flatlands of South Georgia open to rocky outcrops, deep fissures, twenty-foot-high cliffs, and plants found nowhere else in the world.

OPPOSITE: *Drips of watercolor trail down the paper to make the soft reflections of trees and sky seem to float in their own space behind the drawn shapes of the Broxton Rocks formations. Delicate linework creates the beautiful plants growing at the edge of the pool.*

We were headed for the most noted feature of Broxton Rocks—Georgia's southernmost waterfall.

Clambering down the bluffs, we descended into a shallow valley that Frankie explained was the ancient riverbed of the Ocmulgee River. Rocky Creek flowed here now, still carving a path through the rock on its way to join today's Ocmulgee River. As we walked, the cliffs seemed to grow higher on either side. Frankie commented that they were not getting higher; it was an illusion: the riverbed was getting deeper.

A gust of cold air abruptly hit my face; the draft seemed to blow from a fissure in the rock.

I stopped and peered into the dark space. Drops of moisture clung to the cool rock walls, and lichens painted the surrounding stones a bright green and bubblegum pink. Frankie pointed out a nearby crevice partially filled with a drift of dried leaves and other detritus. This was the nest of a wood rat, he said, a species native to the preserve.

The cliffs were cracked in many places, I saw now, and every space was a cool, damp microclimate.

Frankie was mostly quiet as we walked. His eyes scanning, he seemed to concentrate on the life forms around him, a scholar actively observing even now, on a friendly tour. He stopped at a rocky overhang and plucked a green sprig from the cliff wall.

"This is green-fly orchid," he said, holding it out for us to see. "It normally grows on trees, but here it grows right on the rock." He replaced it in a crevice.

Soon we came to the site of the waterfall. The lip of the falls was dry, scattered with last year's leaves, the sound of falling water nowhere to be heard. Before I arrived, Frankie had warned me that, despite recent rains, the ongoing drought had caused the waterfall to temporarily dry up.

Nonetheless, the sandstone boulders massed around the pool below were magnificent. The scene seemed almost a mirage or maybe an oasis lingering from an age long past. Jim and I circled, taking photos, with Jim suggesting different vantages for the best shots. Yet before long, Frankie beckoned us onward—there was much more to see.

We scrambled back up the cliffs to the savannah. Here it was dry, almost desertlike. Frankie pointed to a flat black moss growing on sunbaked rock. It looked dead. "When it rains, this moss will green up within about fifteen minutes," he said. We continued past a shallow mound of sand, which I learned was the apron of a gopher tortoise hole. A sweep of native cane grass was habitat for Bachman's sparrow, a vulnerable species that uses the grassy environment of the longleaf pine savannah for nesting.

Jim pointed out the bright red leaves of sundew, a carnivorous plant that traps insects for food; the plant evolved in nutrient-deficient soils to digest insect proteins for nitrogen. Drifts of wiregrass, golden in winter, waved all around. The sweep of the native grass is a testament to the success of the Nature Conservancy's management of the property: controlled burns to restore plants and wildlife that naturally thrive in this fire-adapted ecosystem. As we conversed, I learned that both Jim and Frankie had been key players in the Nature Conservancy's acquisition of this place. Their advocacy added 1,650 acres to the Broxton Rocks Conservation Area, which now encompasses 13,500 acres.

Jim waved aside my admiration of his efforts and gestured to a sunny opening in the woods—Snow's Glade, he said, a tribute to Frankie and his discoveries.

The afternoon passed in a blur. Frankie knew every plant. At one point he stooped, pocketknife in hand, to pry something from the dirt. Rising, he showed us the reproductive structures of a forb, a herbaceous flowering

plant known as a quillwort. In fact, one quillwort species at Broxton Rocks was unknown until Frankie found it, one of his several discoveries, so it was named Snow's quillwort (*Isoetes snowii*) in his honor.

As we drove out of the preserve, a rather large squirrel with a black and silver mask leaped from tree to tree.

Frankie stopped the car. "That's a Sherman's fox squirrel." We watched him sail through the air, his long tail indeed like a fox's, arching to balance his acrobatics. "He needs the open canopy of the longleaf pine savannah," Frankie said. "He should thrive here now that it's being restored."

As the sun dropped low, we said goodbye to Broxton Rocks, this place to which one man has devoted his life's work, to share its wonders with those who come after.

—A. L.

OPPOSITE: *The grasses of Broxton Rocks swept around Frankie Snow as he led us through the pine savannah. They evoked for me a kind of consuming fire, with Frankie's small figure seeming to fade and rise toward the arch of the sky.*

Broxton Rocks Preserve has been called an ecological and geological island in the vast Atlantic Coastal Plain that includes most of Georgia's southern half. Broxton Rocks is indeed a striking, unique natural wonder amid the otherwise flat sandy terrain of the coastal plain. The region's flatness comes from the sea floor of a primordial ocean that covered most of South Georgia tens of millions of years ago.

The preserve itself is more than fifteen hundred acres amid a longleaf pine forest and various other ecosystems that are part of the larger Broxton Rocks Conservation Area. Because of its outstanding ecological significance, the preserve is accorded special protection that limits public visits to special tours and other arrangements with the conservancy.

Broxton Rocks Preserve's specialness stems from its geology, which creates an unlikely mountain-like landscape that supports numerous floral and faunal oddities, many of them rare. Broxton Rocks essentially is a sandstone rock outcrop, the single largest exposure of sandstone—about four meandering miles—found in what geologists call the Altamaha Formation. The formation is a massive band of subterranean sandstone that underlies fifteen thousand square miles of Georgia's coastal plain.

The preserve area dates from the Middle Miocene era, about thirteen million years ago, as slow erosion from wind, rain, ice, heat, and humidity exposed the sandstone that became Broxton Rocks. Such rock outcrops are uncommon in the coastal plain, making the preserve even more of a phenomenon of nature. The relentless erosion continued for eons—and continues today. A stream, known today as Rocky Creek, formed and over the millennia carved a shallow gorge in the rock that is today the hallmark of the preserve.

Erosion scoured out other remarkable features of Broxton Rocks, including boulders, sandstone cliffs thirty feet high, and cave-like crevices and fractures in rock walls wide enough for a person to walk through. Wide, deep cracks, like those caused by earthquakes, also split the flat surfaces of the outcrop. Today, unwary animals, especially white-tailed deer, occasionally fall into the fissures. Unable to escape, they die.

Rocky Creek, now a tributary of the Ocmulgee River, is also responsible for one of Broxton Rocks's most dramatic features—an enchanting, ten-foot-high waterfall that drops over rock ledges into a scenic pool below. It is Georgia's southernmost waterfall, more characteristic of the Blue Ridge Mountains than the coastal plain flatwoods. In rainy seasons, thousands of gallons of water pass over the ledges every minute, continuously polishing the rocks until they glisten like jewels in the sun. During droughts, the flow may be reduced to a gentle trickle—but remains picturesque.

Together, Rocky Creek, the waterfall, pools, boulders, and network of fissures, cliffs, and crevices create a series of microclimates that keep the gorge and its fissures cool and moist, whereas the conditions on flat rocks above the fissures are almost desertlike. This, in turn, makes Broxton Rocks Preserve a hotspot of biodiversity, hospitable to not only a variety of native Georgia plants but also plants more common to both the tropics and the Appalachian Mountains. In all, the preserve is home to about 530 plant species, more than twenty of them rare, endangered, or unique to Georgia. Scientists from all over the United States come to Broxton Rocks to study this unique array of plant life.

Some plants grow in unusual places at Broxton Rocks. For instance, the epiphytic green-fly orchid, a plant with lustrous green leaves and greenish-yellow flowers, typically grows on trees. But at Broxton Rocks, it adorns the preserve's damp rock walls. Other plants are more typical of tropical climates than South Georgia's. In particular, the grit portulaca, a rare succulent herb, is a native of Cuba but is also found at Broxton Rocks. Scientists speculate that the common nighthawk, a migratory bird that spends winters in Cuba, may eat grit portulaca seeds there and bring them to South Georgia in spring. Another species, the rare shoestring fern, also is found mostly in the southern tropics but grows in moist crevices at Broxton Rocks.

Other rare, endangered, or unusual plants in the preserve include dwarf filmy fern, silky creeping morning glory, Georgia plume, yellow flytrap, and wire-leaf dropseed. In addition, Broxton Rocks is a haven for nonvascular plants, such as mosses, and lichens. Researchers have documented nearly eighty species of mosses there.

Animal-wise, the eastern woodrat, or pack rat, frequently nests among the rocky fissures and boulders. The nocturnal rodent lines its nest with sticks, leaves, bones, pebbles, and other miscellaneous items it comes across.

Several other ecosystems also are part of the Broxton Rocks Preserve—longleaf pine and wiregrass woodlands, hardwood stands, pitcher plant seepage bogs, native grass areas, and others. All contribute to the preserve's remarkable diversity. Diverse animal species inhabit the varied landscape, including the endangered indigo snake, the threatened gopher tortoise, and the imperiled eastern diamondback rattlesnake. More than one hundred bird species have appeared in the preserve, including the endangered red-cockaded woodpecker and the vulnerable, sweet-singing Bachman's sparrow.

The larger Broxton Rocks Conservation Area includes the Flat Tub Wildlife Management Area managed by the Georgia Department of Natural Resources; the Broxton Rocks Forest owned by the Georgia Forestry Commission; and other properties owned by Coffee County and private landowners.

Their collective conservation efforts will preserve the uniqueness and magic of Broxton Rocks well into the future.

—C. S.

10 Ohoopee Dunes

Georgia's desert, sandy glades of elfin oaks and flowers

We got out of the car and donned bright orange vests, purchased from the Walmart in nearby Swainsboro, northwest of Statesboro. It was hunting season at Ohoopee Dunes Wildlife Management Area, and we didn't want to take any chances.

Three friends, Amy, Celeste, and Yasmin, had joined me for this adventure in south-central Georgia. Yesterday we had floated kayaks through the watery world of George L. Smith State Park, marveling at the endless reflections of cypress and tupelo.

This morning we had driven not twenty miles from that forest-in-the-water. Yet we stood now on the edge of what some call "Georgia's desert": a remnant of huge inland dune fields from ages past, perhaps as long as three hundred thousand years ago. The sands blew across the coastal plain from dry riverine beds, accumulating in some places to a height of as much as 120 feet above the floodplain. The result was this strange and magical oasis of sand in the middle of Georgia's pine savannahs.

We set out from the information kiosk at the trail through the McLeod's Bridge Tract. All around us, dry pink sand glittered in the morning sun. We saw no sign of the tall pines typical of the coastal plain. Instead, the ancient

sands had given birth to a diminutive forest of elfin trees—stunted turkey oaks—scrabbling for life in the almost desertlike conditions.

We passed among the trees, miniaturized by the poor soil that meted out water and nutrients in thimblefuls. A small crooked oak along the path caught my eye. Anywhere else, I wouldn't have given a second glance to what appeared to be a young sapling. But the hoary growth of lichen on this tree's narrow trunk betrayed its age. This was no youth. This was an old man, his long years camouflaged by his diminutive size. Here, in this elfin forest, a trunk four to eight inches thick could belong to a wizened denizen, one hundred years old.

The sight of our orange vests was a constant reminder of the possibility of hunters. At one point, Amy halted us to listen—did we hear gunshots? In the fine sand we saw many deer prints. Celeste pointed to the clear footprints of a turkey that crisscrossed the trail with its three-toed hieroglyphics. Animal life seemed abundant here. Soon we came to the mound of a gopher tortoise hole with its characteristic apron of pale sand outside the dark entrance.

OPPOSITE: *A path of dappled sunlight curves through the dwarf oak forest at Ohoopee Dunes. Soft washes of russet and gold create the light sifting through the leaves, while fine ink lines direct the viewer's focus to the tree and clump of wiregrass in the foreground—an invitation to enjoy the craggy surface of the tiny aged oak and the delicate spray of grass beside it.*

Delicate flowers cast bits of color across our path, like confetti from the season's parade of flowers, now passed. Bits of pink gerardia blooms lay scattered among the brown oak leaves. A delicate arch of green, waving flags of bright red blooms, was scarlet wild basil dangling its small bright banners across our path. Orange milkwort held out blossoms on stiff arms, and a bright goldenrod raised its plume high, appearing to salute our passage from its woody flagpole.

I felt the privilege of traveling this rare environment—so fragile yet enduring, sharing with us its small tokens of celebration this late fall morning.

—A. L.

Leaves and bright November flowers scatter across the sand of the dunes, forming small ever-shifting vignettes of color along the trail. Here the blossoms of orange milkwort glow against the rich carpet of oak leaves, threaded with delicate twigs and grasses.

Those who see the Ohoopee Dunes Wildlife Management Area in Emanuel County for the first time may be underwhelmed. At first glance, the protected area may seem nothing more than dull, dry scrubland with stunted, twisted trees and pinkish-white sand that looks more like a harsh desert.

But a closer inspection reveals why botanists and naturalists regard the dunes (about one hundred miles from the ocean) as an enchanting marvel of nature. Despite the site's desertlike appearance, its ancient riverine dunes—rising high above the floodplain of the Little Ohoopee River—harbor some of Georgia's rarest natural communities that support dozens of rare and unique species. The late Georgia naturalist Charles Wharton called the Ohoopee Dunes "one of Georgia's most exceptional, picturesque, and unique" environments. The Nature Conservancy calls it a marvel because of its rarity, diversity, and value to science and education.

The Ohoopee Dunes Wildlife Management Area comprises nine tracts along the Little Ohoopee River in southwestern Emanuel County. Adjacent to the wildlife management area (WMA) are two other tracts—the Ohoopee Dunes Preserve, owned by the Nature Conservancy, and the Covena Tract, owned by the U.S. Fish and Wildlife Service. The Georgia Department of Natural Resources owns the WMA and helps manage the other two tracts. Together the eleven tracts encompass more than ninety-five hundred acres.

The inland dunes are remnants from about three hundred thousand to twelve thousand years ago during glacial periods, when the Little Ohoopee mostly was dry because of severe droughts. The sands were blown up from the dry riverbed onto the river's east bank by westerly winds.

As such, the soil there today is mostly coarse quartz-based sand, identical to the sand that makes up coastal beaches one hundred miles away. Locals refer to the loose, white to pinkish-gray soil as sugar sand. The sandy soil holds few nutrients and drains quickly, which would seem unwelcoming to life. But while the Ohoopee Dunes retain many of the characteristics of beach dunes, thousands of years of weathering by wind, rain, and other natural forces have made the soil hospitable to some of Georgia's rarest and unique plants and animals. In turn, these species add stark notes of beauty and interest to an otherwise harsh environment.

Woody shrubs—several of them rare and unusual—are abundant on the dunes and include sandhill rosemary, woody goldenrod, red basil, Ohoopee Dunes wild basil, blueberry, coastal sweet pepperbush, and others. Conspicuous herbaceous plants of the dunes include gopher apple, sand chickweed, nailwort, wire plant, tread softly, and goat's rue. "It is a striking habitat, with rare evergreens, such as rosemary, and woody mints with colorful blooms as dominant ground cover," Wharton noted in his book *The Natural Environments of Georgia*. They also smell good, he said: "Rosemary and woody mints are not only visually rewarding but olfactorily stimulating."

Ecologists classify most of Ohoopee Dunes' distinct flora as a dwarf oak–evergreen forest, with turkey oaks and dwarf post oaks, clothed in Spanish moss, as the dominant trees. Longleaf pines and live oaks also grow here and there among the dunes. Much of the preserve also is an evergreen scrub–lichen forest. Indeed, it is a haven for lichens, which are curious plantlike organisms formed by symbiotic relationships between fungi and algae. About 150 lichen species have been identified in the eleven tracts of Ohoopee Dunes. Lichens are abundant on the trees, and in some areas they cover the dune surface in thick mats—this is especially true of a species known as reindeer lichen. "The many dwarf trees, unusual shrubs, and white sand strewn with mounded tufts of reindeer lichen give this area a unique character," Hugh Nourse and Carol Nourse write in their book *Favorite Wildflower Walks in Georgia*.

The Ohoopee Dunes' rich assortment of insect life is just as amazing as its floral diversity, drawing many researchers and naturalists there annually. Thousands of insect species inhabit the Ohoopee Dunes. Twenty-two species of grasshoppers and seventy-seven species of ants have been discovered there. Two insect species are believed to occur only in the dunes and nowhere else in the world—the Ohoopee Dunes scarab beetle and the Ohoopee Dunes moth. The moth's larvae use the rare woody goldenrod plant as a food source.

The dunes also are excellent habitat for endangered animals higher on the evolutionary ladder—the gopher tortoise, a protected species in Georgia, and the eastern indigo snake, which is on the federal list of endangered species. The indigo snake often makes its home in gopher tortoise burrows, as do several other creatures.

A looping 1.9-mile trail takes visitors across and around one section of the Ohoopee Dunes WMA, the McLeod's Bridge Tract. Along the way, signs explain the stark environment of the dunes and discuss the flora and fauna of the area and the people who lived and worked there. One sign tells about the role of low-key fire in keeping the scrubby forest healthy by getting rid of unwanted vegetation. Many of the endemic plants and animals that live in the dunes actually depend on occasional controlled burns. Another trail that runs 2.25 miles through the dunes' Hall's Bridge Tract takes visitors through the most scenic and biologically diverse part of the WMA.

Perhaps after walking the trails, a visitor may agree with the naturalists—that this elfin forest and seemingly austere landscape is indeed a land of enchantment.

—C. S.

11 Wade Tract

Old-growth longleaf pines and flowering savannah

"Look at this soil."

Charlie and I watch as Jim Cox thrusts a stick into the ground beneath a pine tree. The stick sinks a good two feet, its end standing like an exclamation point between two soft mounds of wiregrass.

"The soil here is incredibly productive—over forty species of plants can grow in one square meter," Jim says. "Longleaf pine savannah is one of the most species-rich ecosystems in the world."

We're standing knee-deep in a grassy meadow, surrounded with widely spaced pine trees. Sunny glades stretch far into the distance among the trees. This is the Wade Tract Preserve, one of the oldest stands of longleaf pine in the country, in the beautiful rolling Red Hills region of Thomas County. Once it was part of a vast pine savannah that swept the coastal plains from Virginia to Texas. By the 1920s nearly all the longleaf pines had been harvested for timber and the rich soil plowed under for cotton and other crops. But here on the Wade Tract Preserve, the land looks much as it did when Europeans arrived in North America. Today the combined efforts of landowners, management staff, and scientists nurture this grassy woodland of two hundred acres. As a biologist with the nearby Tall Timbers Research Station, which manages the preserve, Jim Cox is an integral part of that effort: he has monitored the health of this site for decades.

OPPOSITE: *Sunbeams sift through the boughs of longleaf pines in this early morning scene at the Wade Tract. Tinted color washes form rainbow prisms in the trees, while dense ink lines create the web of grasses and flowers beneath, flecked with purple liatris and golden partridge peas.*

The air is cool this September morning. The sun streams in long golden bars between the pines. The grass is a sea of yellow blossoms, petals of partridge peas flecked with light swirling around the trees. This airy wood seems less a forest and more a parkland dotted with pines.

I am not prepared for this sweep of peaceful landscape. Pine boughs stir overhead, a whisper in the quiet. A small high-pitched plea, the voice of a bird, floats from above.

"That's a young 'cockaded' begging for food," Jim says.

I'm thrilled. The red-cockaded woodpecker is endangered, making its home in open stands of old pine such as this longleaf pine savannah. Jim trains his binoculars on the treetops. He points to the sparkle of sap on a trunk fifty feet above the ground—a dark shape flutters there, at the scar of a broken branch. "That's not the juvenile—that's an adult red-cockaded. He's beginning an excavation. They only excavate living wood." Longleaf pine is incredibly dense, Jim explains, so the birds have to find wood that has softened. Here, fungus has entered and caused disease.

We take turns with the binoculars, watching the bird circle and prod the trunk.

After a few minutes we get into the truck again; Jim is taking Charlie and me to the next spot. We bump along the primitive dirt road while he unfolds the history of this plantation. Most of the South's grassland fragments, including the Wade Tract, were first preserved by wealthy industrialists of a century ago for quail hunting. They needed the grassland to remain in its natural state because savannah is the quail's favored habitat. This required frequent low-intensity burns like those that occur naturally on the South's coastal plain. Fire kills the underbrush and any young hardwood trees while allowing the longleaf pine and its surrounding community of grassland flowers to flourish. Such flora evolved in a landscape that frequently burns. Tall Timbers Research Station, where Jim works, began as a center for research on restoring this fire-dependent ecosystem.

Jim stops the truck and walks us to a huge pine. Its trunk is a furrowed mosaic of thick fire-blackened bark. "This is the oldest tree on the Wade Tract," he says. It seems a mighty pillar, its branches spreading far overhead. We survey the sooty trunk, so huge that Charlie and Jim together cannot encircle it with their arms. The tree may be more than five hundred years old, maybe more than six hundred, Jim says. A mature longleaf is too hard for drilling a core sample—this tree's age estimate is based on ring counts of comparable fallen trees. He adds that some longleaf pines on the nearby Greenwood Plantation are just as old: trees alive when Columbus arrived in North America. "Longleaf pine is the tree that built America," Jim says. "It was used for everything—ship building, construction. It's a hard, enduring wood and very beautiful."

He has me feel a pointed, fire-blackened stump a few feet away. The protruding spar is rock hard with pitch, as hard as stone or petrified wood.

We circle back to the truck. Next is Greenwood Plantation, and if there is time, perhaps Tall Timbers Research Station as well.

It's hard to leave. This place seems outside the world, a haven from the push and shove of everyday trivialities. Insects hum their soft autumn chorus from the grass, and a bee, tinted blue, adds his descant from the flowers. Yellow sulphur butterflies, wings translucent in the sunlight, flutter a goodbye—or perhaps, they are saying, *Stay, stay.*

The grassland, the gentle sway of the trees in the Wade Tract—the place feels familiar, like a spot where you might plant your cottage and live a long time, maybe always. One could imagine a happily-ever-after here, just sitting in the grass, watching the butterflies, and listening to the birds and the wind, not doing much of anything but *being.*

It feels like home.

—A. L.

The biologist Jim Cox indicates the nest site of a small brown-headed nuthatch. The bird can excavate the dense wood only after the longleaf pine has burned and decay has set in.

In the 1770s, as the famed naturalist William Bartram was traveling across the Southeast during his well-known exploration of the region, he came upon a splendid forest that left him awe-struck. In his book published in 1791, he waxed eloquent at what he saw: "We find ourselves on the entrance of a vast plain which extends west sixty or seventy miles. . . . This plain is mostly a forest of the great long-leaved pine, the earth covered with grass, interspersed with an infinite variety of herbaceous plants, and embellished with extensive savannas, always green, sparkling with ponds of water."

What he was seeing was a slice of the South's majestic longleaf pine forest, which was teeming with life and was truly one of North America's greatest woodland ecosystems when Bartram made his trek. Bartram probably didn't know the full extent of this magnificent system. Estimates vary, but the generally accepted figure is that the longleaf pine ecosystem once covered about sixty million acres in a contiguous, twelve-hundred-mile stretch across nine southern states, Virginia to Texas. Another thirty million acres harbored large longleaf stands mixed with other forest types. The vast majority of this extraordinary system was within the coastal plain, although some expanses were inland.

In Georgia, the longleaf pine forest dominated the landscape of the state's lower half, from the Georgia fall line (a geological boundary that runs from Columbus to Augusta) to the coast. The Spanish conquistador Hernando de Soto and his entourage tromped through this great open forest during their historic march across Georgia in 1540. To the early European settlers who arrived later, longleaf pines were so abundant that they seemed to be an inexhaustible resource.

But that proved not to be the case. Today, across the entire South, less than 3 percent of the region's once-boundless longleaf pine forest remains, found only in scattered remnants across its original range. This is one of the most dramatic declines ever of a once-immense North American ecosystem. Today, the longleaf pine forest is among the continent's most endangered ecosystems. In turn, many creatures that depend heavily on longleaf forests for habitat also have become endangered or threatened—such as the red-cockaded woodpecker, the eastern indigo snake, and the gopher tortoise.

Decades of frenzied cutting cleared the original forest. Because of the high quality of longleaf pine lumber, the trees were in great demand for building houses, ships, and railroads. Huge swaths of the stately pine also disappeared to make way for farmland, urban development, and silviculture. By 1940 most of the longleaf forest was gone and not replaced with new plantings of longleaf. Though the longleaf is superior in quality to other pine species, it grows much more slowly than the others. Foresters and landowners opted to replace the longleafs with faster-growing loblolly and slash pines, which produce faster economic returns.

One other important factor in the longleaf's decline was fire suppression. The longleaf ecosystem is vitally dependent on occasional fires for growth and staying healthy. But as fire suppression became a standard practice among foresters and landowners during the twentieth century, longleaf pines failed to thrive.

Luckily and remarkably, of the longleaf forests that have survived, a handful of them—nearly all on private property—have reached old-age status. Attaining that exalted stage takes the forests two hundred years or more of growth. Today, these old-age remnants offer a glimpse of what the virgin longleaf pine forest looked like in its full glory centuries ago.

Of these old-growth survivors, the best known and most studied are within the Wade Tract. Scientists believe the Wade Tract has remained virtually unchanged since Desoto's time. The U.S. secretary of the interior has designated it a National Natural Landmark.

Without the Wade Tract and perhaps two or three others like it, researchers say, they would have great difficulty understanding the amazing diversity and biological richness of a mature longleaf pine forest. As such, ecologists and conservationists use the Wade Tract as a benchmark for what they ultimately hope to achieve in restoring and managing longleaf pine ecosystems.

Mature longleaf forests are not only eye-pleasing but may be the most biologically diverse North American ecosystems outside the tropics. The groundcover beneath the towering pines may contain as many as three hundred plant species per acre, supporting a multitude of insects, birds, animals, and other creatures, many of them rare and endangered. Scientists have been studying the Wade Tract for decades to understand its amazing biological richness.

Writers, poets, and artists also come to the Wade Tract to celebrate and drink in the forest's stunning beauty. With its stately longleafs in open grassy settings, the Wade Tract looks more like an alluring big-city park than a wild place. Mature longleaf pines—the most distinctive of southern conifers—are splendid trees with straight sturdy trunks rising eighty to one hundred feet or more and dark green, needle-like leaves that are eighteen inches long. The tree takes 100 to 150 years to become full size and may live to be five hundred years old.

The intactness of the Wade Tract and its splendor are testimony to the stewardship of the Wade family, who have long owned the tract and the rest of the ten-thousand-acre Arcadia Plantation. For decades the family allowed their land managers to use prescribed fire to imitate nature and keep the Wade Tract healthy—thereby making it a singularly important site for longleaf ecosystem research.

Now, using the knowledge gained from years of studying and managing the Wade Tract, government agencies, conservation groups, and private and corporate landowners are engaged in intensive efforts to restore longleaf forests on hundreds of thousands of acres across the South. Their hope is that one day the restored forests will resemble the Wade Tract.

—C. S.

12 Providence Canyon

Georgia's Little Grand Canyon

Shall we use the phrase "natural wonder" for a place created by humans?

Providence Canyon in Stewart County is an upstart on Earth's long time line, the result not of geological processes but of the misguided farming practices of settlers in the 1800s. Furrows plowed straight up and down the slopes sent rainwaters hurtling downward, carrying away the fragile layer of topsoil. Furrows became gullies, and the rain washed away the hard cover of clay at the surface, exposing soft white sandstone below.

The land crumbled. Within decades, once-fertile farmland was unusable. What remained was an alien landscape of craggy eroded gullies and fluted canyon-like walls of red and white—a landscape that, ironically, would become the wonder of southwest Georgia.

I called my friend Jennifer, a freelance photographer. Did Georgia's Little Grand Canyon sound like a place she might want to bring her camera?

It did.

Happily, Bill Witherspoon and Leslie Edwards, noted authors of geology and ecology texts, respectively, would be leading a guided tour of the canyon while we were there. Their talks began at noon—an hour that photographers and artists alike shun for its harsh light and shadows. Jennifer and I agreed: we would drive to the park the afternoon before to photograph the canyon

at sunset. I booked rooms at a nearby B&B in Eufala, Alabama, and we set out on a southwesterly course from Atlanta after lunch.

We got there later than we had planned. The day had dawned clear, but by the time we pulled into the park, clouds had gathered, sending dark shadows scurrying over the hills. The entrance sign warned of a sundown closing. I envisioned the gates chained, Jennifer and I trapped in the park all night.

As we hesitated, the sun surged between the clouds, illuminating a distant hilltop. The siren call of light easily triumphed over feeble apprehensions of mere park closings.

I jumped out of the car. "Quick, let's go!"

Jennifer and I half-ran to the Canyon Rim Trail. The nearest overlook revealed the first of the park's sixteen so-called canyons: sandstone walls, waved and sculpted, rising in bands of vibrant orange, bright pink, white, and deep purple. The land undulated in fantastic forms, seeming to defy conventions of geology and even gravity.

We ran from one overlook to the next. The sun had its dalliance, casting our view first in darkness, then in light, as we strained to capture the fleeting moments of sunset in a land already aglow with fiery color.

We ran to the final overlook, perhaps the grandest—chiseled white towers, craggy canyon walls, raw orange and stark white. The sun had dropped low. A dead tree leaned at the cliff's edge, a lonely sacrifice to the continued ravages of the canyon long after the farmers had gone. The landscape was dim, the pale canyon bottom gleaming as a river of sand, its surface frozen in ripples from watery travels down the clay-and-sandstone walls.

As we tarried, the sun made its final farewell, casting rays to every corner of the landscape, illuminating the rocks below. It looked for all the world like a heavenly revelation, a vision of otherworldly glory.

"Look—" Jennifer whispered, "the God light!" Her face lit up, and she raised her camera.

OPPOSITE: *The fiery hues of sunset in Providence Canyon are created here by glazing, a traditional watercolor technique using multiple translucent washes to build intensity of color. The trees in the foreground are rendered with a minimum of line, their forms nearly transparent, so the sunlit ridges can unfold unobstructed—as they appeared to me—rolling away into the horizon.*

We left the park rejuvenated and renewed (and the gates, of course, were standing wide open).

Tomorrow, we'd come down from our nature high and learn about the science of this place. But today, in this barren land, we feasted on something better than food, even better than knowledge: it was the hand of Nature, not of humans, that had made of this place something beautiful.

—A. L.

OPPOSITE: *This painting contrasts starkly with the peaceful sunset on the preceding page. Here I wanted to tell the tale of the violent assault on the land, with raw red pigments and rough brushstrokes tearing across the white of the paper. The sky is dark with clouds. The reds of the clay are spattered almost like blood of the earth, while the white of the paper becomes the canyon's fragile sandstone, which is eroding.*

In about 1830, farmers hell-bent to grow highly lucrative cotton began grabbing up acreage in the rolling terrain of the upper coastal plain of southwest Georgia. The federal government had forced the Creek Indian confederation to cede the land to the United States in the 1825 Treaty of Indian Springs. The farmers quickly put their enslaved laborers to work clear-cutting the native oak, pine, and hickory forests that covered the clay hills, which the farmers believed had the most fertile soils. Soon, the cleared land was blooming white with cotton.

So fervent was the desire to grow the fiber that the farmers pushed their enslaved workers to plow and till the cleared land with little or no regard to protecting the precious soils from erosion. Agriculture reformers at the time suggested that farmers rotate their crops and add manure to the mineral-depleted soils, but the cotton growers paid little heed to such advice. In short order, deep ugly gullies appeared and the loose soil washed away. But the cotton-growing fervor continued. Then, Mother Nature took the upper hand as heavy rains scoured the gullies even wider, deeper, and longer while creating new ones.

By the late 1850s, numerous gullies had become gaping chasms, some so deep and steep that one could easily hide a wagonload of hay—even an entire barn—in them. One big gully was eroding so fast that it sucked up a barn, a schoolhouse, and the graves in a church cemetery. The church itself, Providence Methodist Church, was in imminent danger of toppling into the gorge. Toward the end of the decade, members of the congregation built a new sanctuary at a safer spot farther away and across a road. The huge gully itself became known as Providence Canyon, after the church.

By the 1930s the era of King Cotton was over. But by then Providence Canyon had grown into a spectacular network of gigantic gullies said to resemble rugged badlands out west. What once was a shameful blight on the land had become a sublime sight. People actually started coming from afar to see the amazing, colorful gorges with fanciful shapes. Local boosters saw a chance to lure hordes of tourists and began lobbying Congress to make Providence Canyon a national park, insisting it was natural. Newspapers in Columbus, Atlanta, and other Georgia cities joined the campaign. But Providence Canyon never achieved that lofty status: officials in Washington, D.C., viewed it more as a result of human folly than a creation of nature. In 1971 Providence Canyon had to settle for another kind of distinction: Governor Jimmy Carter's administration made it an official Georgia state park, although the state more recently changed its name to Providence Canyon State Outdoor Recreation Area.

Even so, state park officials today tout Providence Canyon as one of Georgia's Seven Natural Wonders and affectionately call it the state's Little Grand Canyon. It is truly a place of marvel and wonder, although calling it natural and comparing it to the massive world-famous canyon out West—gouged out by a river over millions of years—may be stretching it a bit.

The scenic, 1,009-acre Providence Canyon park actually encompasses a web of sixteen gorges as deep as 150 feet and several hundred yards wide. Several narrow gorges, or finger canyons, branch off from the main canyons. In and around the chasms are breathtaking plateaus, towering cliffs, formations of rock columns, pillars, and sharp pinnacles—all sculpted from erosion of the soft multicolored soils, rocks, and clays. The fragile canyon walls reveal dramatic striped patterns of color, forty-three different hues in all. The purples and pinks derive from manganese in the canyon's sediments, oranges and reds from iron, yellows and tans from limonite, and whites from kaolin.

Providence Canyon also is a botanical treasure, home to hundreds of plant species. Sixteen species of oaks grow in the park. Also in abundance there is the bigleaf magnolia, whose leaves can be twelve inches wide and thirty inches long. The bigleafs, which bloom in spring, sport massive, round, red hairy fruits that look like rose-colored softballs.

The park's botanical gem, however, is a rare native azalea, the plumleaf (*Rhododendron prunifolium*). The red-flowered shrub, which blooms in July and August, exists only in a few counties along the Georgia-Alabama border in the Chattahoochee River Valley, where it lives in ravines and along steep creek banks that also harbor mixed hardwoods and pines. Because of its rarity, the plumleaf azalea, which can grow to ten feet high, is a protected species in Georgia. Providence Canyon harbors more than a thousand plumleaf azaleas, more than anywhere else in the world.

For geologists, soil scientists, and anyone else interested in Earth's history, Providence Canyon is a superb learning place. A hike to the bottom of the canyons is a spectacular trip through time, with each descending step crossing many thousands of years in the geologic record. The park lies in a portion of the coastal plain that was covered sixty to seventy-five million years ago (during the Paleogene Period) by the primordial Atlantic Ocean, which reached as far as the present-day city of Macon. Running water transported sand and clay particles, or sediments, from the uplands and deposited them in riverbeds, along shorelines, and in shallow ocean bottoms. When sea levels fell and the ocean retreated, the sediments were exposed as dry land. Millions of years later, these sediments suffered massive erosion from destructive farming; what remained were the deep gullies of Providence Canyon.

The canyon is still changing, still being worn away by the relentless forces of nature. Erosion from heavy rains will continue to enlarge the gorges and threaten the collapse of canyon rims and walls for decades to come. Pinnacles will get smaller and perhaps disappear altogether. Geologists say large amounts of sediments in canyon walls can suddenly come crashing down, a process known as mass wasting, and form the fan-shaped deposits called talus cones.

Some, however, view Providence Canyon with great irony. "On its surface . . . Providence Canyon State Park could well be the nation's most ironic conservation area," writes the historian Paul S. Sutter in his book *Let Us Now Praise Famous Gullies*. He is a former University of Georgia professor. There is irony, he notes, in a park that celebrates the natural results of human-induced soil erosion. "It is difficult to get past the irony of Providence Canyon: the incongruity of, even the humor in, the granting of park status to a network of massive erosion gullies," he writes.

Even so, Providence Canyon is a sight to see. But it also should be a reminder of the terrible consequences of humans' unwise interference with nature.

—C. S.

13 Doerun Pitcher Plant Bog

Lush colony of carnivorous plants

Six times I watched lightning rip the clouds. I stared through my windshield as a wall of black thunderheads boiled up. The roadside fields glowed with a yellow light. It looked like tornado weather.

I considered turning around. But Doerun Pitcher Plant Bog in Colquitt County was not even ten miles away. And a voice in my head offered hopefully that the storm might break or blow east. Besides, it was midsummer, so I still had two hours before dark.

So I continued on the two-lane country byway. Before long I was turning into the narrow dirt road at the entrance sign, DOERUN PITCHER PLANT BOG WILDLIFE MANAGEMENT AREA, named for the carnivorous plants whose leaves form a pitcher-shaped trap.

Bang!

The roof of my truck rang with the impact. Something large. Bang! Bang! These noises were alarming. Pine trees? I pictured branches dropping in the wind that had suddenly kicked up.

But it wasn't the wind—it was hail.

Rocks of ice bounced off the hood. Through the side window I could see hailstones, of the proverbial golf ball size, collecting in the long wiregrass. My ears rang as a particularly large one hit the door. I looked out through

the streaming windows. All I could see were longleaf pines on either side, impossibly tall and widely spaced. No shelter.

Feeling a bit foolhardy, I stopped the truck. If a tornado came roaring through, I wasn't sure I would even hear it.

The hail was probably denting the hood. It served me right—trying to squeeze in this visit, an impromptu detour from I-75 on a return trip from Florida. I had ignored half the weather forecast—a cloud symbol, complete with lightning bolt—and had focused on the precipitation prediction—supposedly just 30 percent.

I couldn't imagine what the hail was doing to the pitcher plants. Their tall green columns would be broken and leaning by now. This was a war zone. So much for getting great photos.

On the other hand, I thought philosophically, I was experiencing firsthand a typical summer storm on Georgia's coastal plain. Without humans' intervention, lightning would kindle wildfires that raced across the wiregrass. I squinted at the blackened trunks of the pines. Frequent controlled burns had left the trees undamaged but had cleared the undergrowth that would otherwise have displaced the bog's unique and beautiful flowers, including the pitcher plants'.

The hail subsided, the barrage over. I stepped into a soft rain that seemed to weep on the broken flowers scattered in the grass. Stokes aster, a purple thistle, gold coneflower—all down, stems bowed to the ground.

And where had the wild creatures gone in the storm?

I picked my way along the trail, an obstacle course of puddles and grass clumps, until I reached the wooden platform that overlooks the bog. I braced myself for ruin.

But tall and bright, yellow pitcher plants rose unbroken from the bog. They stood two feet, even three feet, high, their columns smooth and whole.

OPPOSITE: *Glowing columns of pitcher plants recede swiftly into the shadows of the Doerun bog. The mass of their forms, thrusting down into the picture plane, echoes the energy of the summer storm that was pounding the grasses around them.*

Hailstones lay everywhere, but the plants seemed unscathed. What botanical armor allowed them to stand when all else was laid low?

What's more, they were thriving on soggy ground poor in nitrogen. Pitcher plants capture nutrients in the form of insects. The plants' tall emerald carafes, shapely and fragrant, whisper to the insects, *Come, drink, and taste of my marvelous brew*. A slippery inner wall and downward-pointing hairs trap the bugs in a deadly pool of enzymes at the bottom. There, instead of eating, they are eaten.

At the base of the pitcher plants, I noticed carnivorous companions—small sundews clustered in crimson starbursts. Their leafy pads sparkled with tiny diamond droplets, sweet but sticky. Together with the pitcher plants, they laid a mesmerizing table for the unwary, a feast beautiful but deadly.

I walked back to the truck. It was getting dark. I stood a moment to listen. The forest creatures were beginning to stir again. From the trees came the squeak of a brown-headed nuthatch and the coos of a wood dove. These 650 acres, I knew, were also home to quail, gopher tortoise, and turkey—and many other creatures that remained hidden. Each had learned to survive in this beautiful but sometimes brutal place.

I would retreat for the night to my truck, hotel, and pillowy bed. But these creatures of nature, whether leafed, feathered, or furred, would continue here through lightning, fire, and hail.

Perfectly made to not just survive but to flourish.

—A. L.

As its name implies, the Doerun Pitcher Plant Bog Wildlife Management Area is a sanctuary for pitcher plants, some of the world's most fascinating flora, that make meals by luring, trapping, and consuming flies, gnats, midges, beetles, and other small creatures.

Pitcher plants and other flesh-eating flora—including bladderworts, butterworts, sundews, and the Venus flytrap—live in wetlands known as bogs, several types of which occur worldwide. The Doerun bogs, which lie amid open, hilly pinelands deep in southwest Georgia, are seepage bogs—often called pitcher plant bogs because of their most conspicuous inhabitants. Great swaths of these natural systems once covered the coastal plain of the southeastern United States. Only about 3 percent of these systems survive; the rest were lost to development, pesticide misuse, and fire suppression. (Fire keeps the bogs open and free of invasive vegetation.) All pitcher plants in Georgia are protected; some are listed as threatened or endangered.

Doerun is home to one of Georgia's largest remaining pitcher plant complexes and the state's principal example of these fascinating ecosystems. Flourishing in a hundred-acre portion of the Doerun Wildlife Management Area (WMA) are wide expanses of the trumpet-shaped plants whose striking floral displays are marvelous at almost any time of year.

Pitcher plants belong to the genus *Sarracenia*, which comprises eight species in the United States. Seven are confined to the coastal plain of the southeastern United States, including Georgia. At Doerun, three species grow in lush profusion—the parrot, hooded, and yellow trumpet (or yellow flytrap) pitcher plants. The pitchers, which are actually modified leaves, emerge from branching underground rhizomes. Of the three species, the yellow trumpet is the showiest, at nearly three feet high. The six-inch parrot pitcher plant is the smallest, and the hooded pitcher plant can grow to twice that height.

Seepage bogs usually occur in sunny low-lying areas of rolling pinelands on the coastal plain. Seepage results from the percolation of water from adjacent uplands into porous layers of soil at the base of the hills. The soil—usually sandy and covered with thin layers of peat or sphagnum—is underlain with impermeable layers of clay or limestone rock and remains soggy for most of the year.

Two other important features are characteristic of bog soil—acidity and a deficiency in nutrients, conditions too harsh for many plants. But like other photosynthetic green plants, pitcher plants also need nutrients such as nitrogen to thrive. Most plants absorb nutrients through their roots from nutrient-rich soil. But since pitcher plants and other carnivorous plants live in bogs where nutrients are scarce, they evolved to obtain the essential nutrients by feasting on insects and other small creatures.

Pitcher plants, however, try to avoid eating some insects—including several bees and flies that spread pollen from plant to plant. Like numerous other flowering plants, pitcher plants rely on insect pollinators to reproduce and procreate their species. As such, the plants have evolved mechanisms to help their pollinators avoid being ensnared in the pitchers. For example, the flowers of pitcher plants are located above their traps. The flowers produce pollen and nectar that attract pollinators and different scents and color patterns to lure prey.

Pitcher plants, though, are not the only plants that call seepage bogs home. Despite the bogs' tough conditions, they are places of notable biodiversity. Some other acid-tolerant plants, including grasses, sedges, and several wildflower species, manage to thrive there. Several are endangered or of "special concern" because of their rarity and threats to their survival. Seepage bogs are often regarded as especially hospitable to colorful wild orchids; Doerun is home to several such species—small spreading pogonia, common grass pink, rose pogonia, yellow-fringed orchid, small white-fringed orchid, and a few species of ladies' tresses. Other commonly encountered species include meadow beauties, bog buttons, pipeworts, yellow-eyed grasses, hatpins, colicroot, bog gentians, and milkworts. When these plants bloom together, the bogs can be some of the showiest natural gardens in Georgia's coastal plain.

But some plants that tend to make their way into pitcher plants are unwelcome. These include woody shrubs like gallberry, wax myrtle, bayberry, and fetterbush. If left unchecked, these species can dominate seepage bogs and eventually choke out the pitcher plants and other herbaceous species. For eons frequent lightning-set fires kept woody shrubs at bay and maintained bogs as open habitats, allowing pitcher plants and other sun-loving herbaceous plants to abound. Today at Doerun, biologists keep the bogs healthy by using prescribed burning and occasional mowing.

Before the State of Georgia acquired the Doerun natural area in 1994, it had been lovingly cared for by its owners, Ann and Tommy Barber of Moultrie, who managed it for quail hunting. The couple used prescribed burning and other methods to keep the property healthy and in its natural state, making it a treasured hotspot of natural splendor. Occasionally, the Barbers invited plant lovers to explore the pitcher plant bogs and the surrounding forest. After the state bought the 650-acre tract from the couple, then-governor Zell Miller designated it as a state heritage preserve in 1996. The designation required that the property be kept in its natural condition and used primarily for research, education, and low-impact recreation.

For visitors who want to see this remarkable place, a half-mile nature trail begins at the kiosk with self-guided side trails to a platform that provides an overview of a pitcher plant bog and has loop trails to other bogs and uplands.

—C. S.

14 Pine Mountain

Mountain laurel, waterfalls, and vistas from Georgia's southernmost peak

It's the dark hour before sunrise when I start the drive to Pine Mountain. Located two hours south and west of Atlanta, Pine Mountain is the highest peak in a small and ancient mountain range bordering Georgia's coastal plain, and it is the southernmost mountain east of the Mississippi.

The exact timing of my visit—late April—is a recommendation from Jim Hall of the Pine Mountain Trail Association. His group's robust Facebook page gave me a place for my questions, and I received an almost immediate response from him. To my delight, he even included his mobile number.

When I phoned, however, Jim's answer was abrupt. "Call back in an hour."

As it turned out, Jim was getting a blood transfusion for a knee surgery; his dedication was in evidence—he called back as soon as the nurse had finished. He appreciated hearing that Charlie Seabrook's list of wonders mentioned the spectacular view from the peak of Pine Mountain, called Dowdell's Knob. I asked Jim when he would recommend that I visit.

"Well . . . the most popular time to come is in the fall," he said. "The view from Dowdell's Knob when all the trees are turning is really nice." He paused. "But my personal opinion? I think the prettiest time is the spring, on the Wolfden Loop. It's full of all the mountain laurel blooming . . ." His voice trailed off as though words failed him. He finished: "I just think it's really special."

OPPOSITE: *Mountain laurel crowns Wolfden Trail on Pine Mountain with clouds of pink and white in May. The scene evoked for me a Monet landscape, with the edges of the blossoms and foliage dissolving into the light. Cool dark greens offer the eye the main clue to shape and form, indicating the shadow side of the mountain laurels bordering the path.*

My ears perked up: an insider tip.

Jim directed me to a short section of Pine Mountain Trail. Two miles—or four miles total—from the WJSP-TV tower to Cascade Falls and back, he said, would give me the best of the mountain laurel display. What's more, he promised to monitor the developing blooms and alert me when peak bloom time got close—probably sometime in late April.

Thus the last Saturday of April finds me pulling in next to the WJSP-TV tower at midmorning. Only two other cars are parked in the lot; maybe I'll have the mountain to myself.

The landscape at the trail entrance is unimpressive. The woods are thin, the trail bordered with weedy growth. I feel a twinge of doubt—did I make a mistake and miss the early morning view from Dowdell's Knob?

But just a few minutes' walk brings larger trees into view. The air changes, becoming cooler and moister, the shadows deepen almost imperceptibly.

And then I am in a forest. A beautiful, breathing forest in spring. Birds trill around me—the towhee, the Carolina wren, and others I cannot identify. The voice of the stream calls from the hollow beside the trail. The song is blended and ever changing, the music of water tumbling over rocks and dropping to deep pools, complex and multitoned. It is almost the sound, or the echo, of someone speaking or singing.

The stream is Wolfden Branch. Her path keeps company with the trail, and now her voice follows me as I walk the morning woods.

Soon the mountain laurel peeps through the branches along the trail. It floats in clouds of white and pink through the leafy woods, sunbeams sifting through multistoried layers, the masses of flowers so thick that they meet overhead. I walk through a tunnel of sunlight and blossoms, a great bridal bower of flowers and spring. This forest is one of light.

I shake my head. I do not understand why I am the only human here. And yet, surrounded by beauty, I do not feel alone.

No other traveler has appeared as I reach the turnaround point at Cascade Falls. The stream lilts and chatters, falling twenty feet into a clear pool. I climb a small cliff to the side and dangle over the edge, hanging onto a small tree as I poke my camera through the mountain laurel and photograph the falls.

The high rocky ledge makes a good seat. As I look down on the water, I sit to enjoy my drink and a granola bar. After a while, a hiker arrives and sits by the pool below, then a small troop of scouts. A family with children joins them, splashing in the water under the cascade.

They don't see me in this hidden spot above the rocks.

After they leave, I climb down. I walk back to my car the way I came, slowly, and then I take the road to the top of the mountain to see Dowdell's Knob after all: a sweeping vista, a great dome of blue sky and shining clouds. Wrapping the peak is a meadow of blooming ragwort and blue tradescantia (spiderwort), blanketing the slope with billows of gold and blue. The shadows of clouds race across the flowers and then over the valley far, far below.

I decide I will come back to see the peak in the fall. But I will miss my spring companions—the April sun, the flowers, and the voice of the stream.

—A. L.

Blue-flowered spiderwort blooms amid fields of golden ragwort on the peak of Dowdell's Knob. The horizon stretches far into the distance.

This painting explores the intricate architecture of the tree and its surrounding lattice of mountain laurel. Warm orange on the textured bark conveys the intensity of reflected light from the trail.

A page in my sketchbook from Pine Mountain.

One of Georgia's most unusual mountains, Pine Mountain, is where you wouldn't expect a mountain to be—in Middle Georgia, about 150 miles south of the much larger and better known Appalachian Mountains, whose peaks, ridges, and valleys dominate most of North Georgia's landscape. Pine Mountain is a natural phenomenon all its own, geologically distinct from the Appalachians. It lies about eighty miles southwest of Atlanta, near where the rolling Piedmont region meets up with the flat sandy coastal plain.

Occupying most of Pine Mountain is the 9,049-acre Franklin D. Roosevelt State Park, Georgia's largest state park. With its series of tumbling waterfalls, gurgling brooks, breathtaking mountain vistas, and lush, mossy, leafy forests, the park has become a major southern landmark, one of the most beautiful natural areas in the Deep South.

Pine Mountain, named for the longleaf pines growing on its ridges, actually is a mountain range that begins near the Chattahoochee River to the west and stretches east about twenty miles through Harris, Meriwether, and Talbot Counties. For much of its length, its elevation exceeds one thousand feet, reaching its highest point at a historic peak known as Dowdell's Knob. At 1,395 feet above sea level, Dowdell's Knob is the southernmost peak in the eastern United States. Pine Mountain's eastern half peters out at Sprewell Bluff (chapter 18), a scenic, rugged section of the Flint River. At the bluff, the river bisects the mountain, creating a sheer cliff that drops nearly four hundred feet to the river.

For centuries, geologists, biologists—and writers and poets—have pondered why a mountain range would exist in Middle Georgia. They have concluded that millions of years ago geological forces—faulting, folding, and plate tectonics—in that area thrust up the mountain. Underlying it mostly is Hollis quartzite, an extremely hard metamorphic rock formed from sandstone laid down on the primordial ocean bottom and altered by immense heat and pressure beginning 250 million years ago.

It is fitting that the splendid state park atop Pine Mountain was named for Franklin Roosevelt, the nation's thirty-second president. About eight years before he was elected president in 1932, Roosevelt had been seeking relief for his polio-paralyzed legs at Warm Springs near Pine Mountain. Warm Springs's therapeutic pools of naturally warm, mineral-laden water soothed his aching limbs (chapter 15). While there, he quickly fell in love with the bold steep slopes and scenic vistas of Pine Mountain and would go out on daytime drives to explore the area.

He liked Pine Mountain so much that he returned many times after he became president, not only for therapy but also to escape the intense stress of Washington. His famous getaway cottage in Warm Springs, the Little White House, sits in the shadow of Pine Mountain. On the mountain itself, his favorite place was Dowdell's Knob and its magnificent view of the peaceful valley below. He had a stone barbecue grill and seating built at the overlook, which became a favorite picnic spot for him and his friends, family members, and visiting dignitaries. But he often spent hours alone at the overlook, which granted him precious peace and solitude as he contemplated the awesome task of guiding the nation through the dark days of the Great Depression and World War II.

Roosevelt died in April 1945 at the Little White House from a cerebral hemorrhage. But years before his death, he had laid careful plans for ordinary people to also enjoy the beauty and tranquility of Pine Mountain. The result was the state park, its trails, features, and buildings built in 1935 by his administration's Civilian Conservation Corps, part of his New Deal policies. Among the features constructed by the young men of the CCC were the Liberty Bell Pool and the fifteen-acre Lake Delanor, a reservoir, and its companion, the twenty-five-acre Lake Franklin. The park originally was named Pine Mountain State Park but later was renamed F. D. Roosevelt State Park. Because of the well-preserved CCC design, layout, and buildings of the park, and for its association with Roosevelt, in 1997 the U.S. secretary of the interior designated the area a National Historic Landmark District.

Although Roosevelt was a great nature lover, he probably did not fully realize Pine Mountain's significance as a botanical and ecological gem. Because of its location between the edges of the Piedmont and the coastal plain, the mountain range is a geographical crossroads. Its variety of habitats—dry ridgetops, moist valleys, savannah-like openings, springs, perennial streams, and small glades—supports a mixture of plants familiar to more northerly climes growing side by side with plants of the coastal plain. On Pine Mountain, for instance, mountain laurel amazingly grows right next to titi, a coastal plain shrub.

The ridgetops harbor stands of the longleaf pine that give the mountain its name. On a slope stands a small grove of American chestnuts, a remnant of the great chestnut forest that once covered the eastern seaboard.

Today the park is crisscrossed by an extensive, well-maintained trail system offering plenty of options for seeing the park's array of ecological and historical riches. One walking route is the twenty-three-mile Pine Mountain Trail that has accesses at many different points as it traverses the park. Another trail is the popular 4.3-mile Dowdell's Knob Loop, which begins at the overlook that so enthralled Roosevelt. The sweeping view from there is still much the same as he saw it. The barbecue grill built for his cookouts also is still there. In 2007 the State of Georgia erected a sculpture of Roosevelt seated at Dowdell's Knob and gazing out at the glorious view he loved so dearly.

—C. S.

15 Warm Springs

Soothing spring waters naturally warmed by the earth

After spending the morning on Pine Mountain, I headed for the historic district of Warm Springs, which is practically next door to the park. I wanted to explore this Georgia wonder for the afternoon.

The site turned out to be a collection of buildings—Roosevelt's Little White House, two small cottages, a gift shop, and the Historic Pools Museum. I headed for the museum—what would I see?

A small basin in the museum captures a flow of spring water as it is piped in, inviting visitors to feel the temperature. I learned the water bubbles from the earth at a constant 88 degrees Fahrenheit—nine hundred gallons a minute. It was long reputed to have healing properties: by 1832 a resort had risen around the site. The springs' most famous visitor, Franklin Roosevelt, came as a young man to recover after a crippling bout with polio, and he returned periodically until his death. The Little White House was his home when he visited.

Every turn of the springs' historic tale has been painstakingly documented. But as a natural wonder, it seemed to me to have been diminished, amputated from its roots in the natural world.

I approached one of the museum guards in his dark uniform. Were there any trails on the grounds where I might see some of the springs in a natural setting?

Well . . . not really, he said.

I explained I was an artist and wanted to paint the landscape of the springs.

He thought a minute. “Well, there are places out back where the warm water still bubbles up.” He indicated the wooded grounds behind the building. “It’s not really open to the public, but you go ahead and walk back there—you might find some places.”

Gratefully, I trekked around the building and into the small woods, thick with leaves. Before long I found dampness, a puddle on the forest floor. I knelt to feel the water—it was warm!

The springs were still here, living waters in the landscape.

I swept the leaves aside to see the water coming up. Too late, I saw the salamander. The next instant he was gone.

The quiet spot invited reverie. What was here before the waters were captured and corralled? Did the warm pools harbor plants or creatures that otherwise lived far south? Had the Indians beheld an oasis that glowed turquoise and steamed in the winter?

I hoped the descendants of the little salamander would remain to grace this wonder with their presence.

—A. L.

The naturally heated water of Warm Springs in Meriwether County in Central Georgia flows from the most famous and historic springs in the state—historic for their enduring connection to President Franklin D. Roosevelt.

Shortly before he was elected to the Oval Office in 1932, he had built his own six-room cottage at Warm Springs for his visits to the therapeutic waters.

The water itself, however, is what makes Warm Springs a natural treasure. It's why Georgia tourism officials list Warm Springs as one of the state's Seven Natural Wonders. Its magic begins with ordinary rain falling on the crests of nearby Pine Mountain (chapter 14). The rainwater infiltrates the soil and percolates through cracks in the underlying quartzite rock to a depth of about thirty-eight hundred feet. There, heat generated naturally by the Earth's core warms the water to 88 degrees Fahrenheit—about the temperature of bath water. Natural artesian pressure forces the water to the surface, where it gushes at a rate of about nine hundred gallons per minute, still at 88 degrees. Laboratory tests have shown that the heated water, on its ascent to the top, is enriched with calcium, magnesium, silica, and other minerals, mostly because water at high temperatures dissolves more minerals and dissolves them faster than cold water.

However, scientists debate the medicinal benefits of these minerals. For decades many people have claimed that the water's various minerals can bring relief from a wide range of ills, including gout, diabetes, eczema, syphilis, rheumatism, stomach ailments, and even cancer. Scientific studies dispute that, saying that the water's natural buoyancy and the exercise from swimming in it may be most responsible for the feel-good effects. Even so, untold numbers of people have been drawn to Warm Springs for centuries because of their strong belief that the warm mineral-laden water has mystical healing powers.

When Roosevelt first visited Warm Springs in 1924, he was seeking a cure for the polio that had afflicted him three years earlier. The buoyant spring water brought him no miracle cure, but it did bring significant improvement, which drew him back to the springs time after time until his death.

But long before European settlers found Warm Springs, Native Americans believed in the water's curative properties. They brought their sick and wounded to the springs to bathe in the water—and drink it—and lie in the warm mud. Warm Springs at that time lay within the territory of the Creek

Indians, who peacefully allowed other tribes to bring their ailing people to the springs. Among them were Iroquois from as far as what is now New York State. They called the Creeks' territory "the land where the waters are warm." The Creeks, though, were forced to give up their land in Georgia under the 1825 Treaty of Indian Springs.

As European settlers moved into Georgia, word spread about the healing qualities of the warm spring waters. Soon the town of Bullochville, which later changed its name to Warm Springs, sprang up nearby. In 1832 a local entrepreneur built the first resort for two hundred guests on the site of the warm springs. The resort prospered until 1869 when it was gutted by fire, but it was soon rebuilt. In 1893 Charles Davis built an impressive Victorian-style resort called the Meriwether Inn that could accommodate three hundred guests. It also featured tennis courts, bowling alleys, and trap-shooting ranges. The springs underwent even more development with the completion of several pools that brimmed with the warm spring water.

But around the turn of the century, when the automobile gave people more choices of vacation spots, the resort started to decline. By 1923 it had become badly dilapidated—although people continued to use the springs. The following year, after experiencing the invigorating effects of warm springs, Roosevelt bought the inn and a seventeen-hundred-acre farm close by. Three years later, he founded the Georgia Warm Springs Foundation to help other polio victims. Roosevelt's money paid for construction of many of the treatment pools, which transformed the springs into a "hydrotherapeutic treatment" center to alleviate the debilitating effects of polio. An outdoor pool for the public also was added.

In 1942, however, the treatment pools were supplanted by an indoor pool built on the foundation's adjacent campus because of the difficulty of moving patients to the outdoor pools. The outdoor pools became mostly for recreation and occasional treatment, but during the 1960s, with costs mounting rapidly to maintain them, the state drained and closed the pools. The Georgia Department of Natural Resources later stabilized and partially renovated the springs and pool complex in 1994–1995 to commemorate the fiftieth anniversary of Roosevelt's death and reopened the pools to the public on special occasions. But the pools later were closed again after cracks and other problems were found.

Since then, more work has been done to preserve Warm Springs' historic legacy and to celebrate its natural attributes. The state now manages the historic pools and surrounding structures as a museum. A touch pool allows visitors to dip their fingers in the warm spring water and listen to information about its history. A preservation goal is to return the pools to their former glory—and make them once again a place where people with disabilities can get relief from water warmed and enriched by nature.

—C. S.

16 Oaky Woods

Ancient seabeds, blooming prairie, and black bear haven

I climbed into John Trussell's old truck. On the floor at my feet I spied a pile of what looked like misshapen rocks.

"This is a fossilized whale vertebra," John said as he reached a long arm over to pick up one of the lumps and hand it to me. It did look like a huge vertebra. He put the truck in gear and we were off. John narrated along the way.

"Where we're going we'll find sea fossils from around a hundred million years ago, when half of Georgia was under the ocean," he said.

We were nowhere near the coast.

Oaky Woods Wildlife Management Area is a thirteen-thousand-acre wilderness just south of Macon, smack in Middle Georgia. When I called the field office to plan my visit, John, a retired law enforcement officer and longtime outdoor enthusiast, had responded right away. Silver haired, tall, and energetic, he doesn't project "retired." When he found out I planned to write about this place, he immediately volunteered to give me a personal tour.

If there is such a thing as a guardian spirit of a place, John Trussell is that for Oaky Woods.

Born and raised here, he became a champion for its preservation in the 1980s. Later, he forged a partnership of locals, politicians, and conservationists and spearheaded the "Save Oaky Woods" campaign that eventually led

to the state's land purchase in 2010 that created the Oaky Woods Wildlife Management Area.

To visit Oaky Woods is to walk through a hundred million years of natural history. Embedded in its vast acres are a combination of treasures found nowhere else on Earth: pockets of rare blackland prairie with its unique wildflowers, crumbling bluffs of ancient sea fossils from the Cretaceous period, and the largest black bear population between the Blue Ridge Mountains and Okefenokee Swamp. Wildlife biologists estimate that more than three hundred black bears live in Oaky Woods.

John seemed to know every nook. We hiked to the ocean fossil beds among the pines and found in almost every rock the impression of a mollusk or sand dollar. Farther on were the remains of a century-old still from Prohibition days, its huge vat ruined in an explosion. The lid had landed across the stream. We stopped beside the water to inspect the animal tracks and to stand inside Old Sequoia, a pine with a hollow large enough to hold a man.

John said he had given this tour perhaps hundreds of times—for scouts, hiking clubs, and conservation groups.

Finally, we emerged from the woods in a wide open area—the blackland prairie. Here a rare combination of elements in the soil supports a community of plants found in only a few other places in the world. Blooming under the sun were acres of goldenrod, blue aster, and billowing pink clouds of native grass in full bloom. I had never seen this in the wild.

Driving out, we climbed the one hundred feet to the top of a historic fire tower, where rangers once kept watch during fire season. From the top we could see miles of forest all around.

John related one last story, about a group that had called him from the Flint River area. "They said, 'We want you to lead our effort to save this

John Trussell holds the fossils of a sand dollar and a coral, both from the Cretaceous period.

OPPOSITE: *In September, the rare blackland prairie at Oaky Woods blazes with color. Here the white of the paper becomes a country road, leading the viewer into a detailed pen-and-ink landscape inspired by Rembrandt etchings. Colorful washes sweep across the painting from the left, showing blooming grasses and goldenrod. Fine lines scratched with a knife create the stems of the long grasses.*

Georgia aster mingles with plumes of goldenrod on the Oaky Woods prairie. Glorious color is the focus here, with delicate pen lines helping the eye to find the purple aster amid the masses of goldenrod. A glimpse of a native bee emerges at the far right, working the flowers for pollen.

place, like you did Oaky Woods.' I told them I could give them pointers—but the effort can't come from an outsider. 'That's your place—I can tell you how to do it, but it needs to be you.'"

John said that many, many people worked to save this piece of Middle Georgia for posterity. But when I left that day, I had no doubt that this gift to Georgia—its people and its wild creatures—would not have happened without the love and efforts of this one man, John Trussell—Oaky Woods's guardian spirit.

—A. L.

Of all the rare unique habitats that make Oaky Woods Wildlife Management Area a botanical sanctuary, its most exceptional habitats are small grasslands known as blackland prairies. More than 260 species of wildflowers, native grasses, and other herbaceous plants grow in the prairies. Some are the same species found on western prairies. Several are critically endangered in Georgia.

Leading botanists call the prairies globally rare habitats. Because of its biological significance, the Oaky Woods Wildlife Management Area also is designated a state natural heritage preserve. Established by the Georgia General Assembly, the Heritage Act preserves "certain real properties" that, among other things, exhibit "unique natural characteristics."

Oaky Woods's prairies are remnants of the blackland prairie region (so named because of the dark surface colors of the soil) that stretched in a narrow crescent through Alabama and Mississippi with patches in Georgia and Tennessee. The region once encompassed more than 350,000 acres, but most of it was converted to farmland, pine plantations, and other uses. Estimates are that only about one percent remains.

In Georgia, botanists now know of—and have studied—at least a dozen of these remnant grasslands, ranging from about two to twenty acres in Houston, Twiggs, Bleckley, and Peach Counties. Most of them, however, are concentrated in the rolling terrain of Oaky Woods in southeast Houston County.

The peculiar chalky, clay-rich soil is what makes the prairies so unusual. The soil had its origins ages ago in the late Cretaceous and Eocene geologic periods (66–30 million years ago). During that time, a shallow, primordial sea covered the bottom half of Georgia and much of the rest of the Southeast. In Georgia, the sea's shoreline stretched across what is now the middle of the state—about 150 miles from the shore of the Atlantic Ocean today. (Proof that the shoreline once existed in Middle Georgia comes from abundant marine fossils—sharks' teeth, whale bones, seashells—found in an ancient ridge and other areas in Oaky Woods.)

During the millions of years, shells and exoskeletons of marine creatures rich in calcium carbonate accumulated at the seashore and geologic processes eventually transformed the material into limestone and chalk, a soft form of limestone. Feldspar washing down from the Piedmont formed an alkaline clay and mixed with the limestone. The mixture was weathered down into several soil types, including the kind that eventually became fertile blackland prairie soil.

A particularly distinctive trait of the mineral-laden soil helps keep the grasslands intact: the soil shrinks and swells with moisture. When wet, it expands and becomes sticky, able to bog even a four-wheel-drive pickup. When dry, it turns hard and crumbly, even powdery. The result of this shrink-swell effect is that it retards the growth of trees and other woody plants but allows herbaceous (nonwoody) grasses and wildflowers to flourish. In addition, the alkaline soil, which favors the growth of grasses, and occasional fire also keep the woody plants in check.

In July, the prairies of Oaky Woods can be a stunning riot of blooming wildflowers, particularly the yellow prairie coneflower, one of the grasslands' signature plants. Its bright yellow blooms make the grasslands glow. Later in the season, various asters and grasses are highly visible, including hairgrass, eastern gray goldenrod, and New England aster. During the fall the rare Georgia aster grows along the edges of the prairies.

Although the blackland prairies may be Oaky Woods's natural showcases, the wildlife management area is home to other unique and biologically important habitats that host hundreds of other plant species and engender the adoration of botanists and conservationists. The habitats include limestone bluff forests, limestone bottomland forests, mesic slope (moderately moist) forests, and others. All are related to the blackland prairies, according to botanists. Like the prairies, the fertility and diversity of these habitats stem in large part from the soils derived from the weathering of limestone and chalk.

Befitting its name, Oaky Woods contains an astounding mix of fifteen oak species—Shumard, Durand, swamp chestnut, chinquapin, cherrybark, water, black, laurel, white, overcup, blackjack, northern red, southern red, willow, and post oaks. Botanists say that the presence of the rare Durand oak alone makes Oaky Woods unique. Georgia's largest population of the limestone-loving tree (named for Elias Durand, a nineteenth-century American botanist) is found in Oaky Woods. Some individuals are the largest of their species in the United States.

Together, the diverse habitats support an array of native creatures, making Oaky Woods one of Georgia's most important wildlife havens. That includes an environment wild enough for black bears to roam. Oaky Woods and neighboring lands support one of Georgia's three major bear populations. The black bear is the state's only bear species.

The bears, the blackland prairies, and the other unique habitats of Oaky Woods all contribute to Georgia's amazing biological diversity, a natural legacy that future generations of Georgians will inherit.

—C. S.

17 George L. Smith State Park

Pond mirrors vivid orange-bronze cypress in fall

The cypress trees stand knee deep in the dark tea-colored water. Moss hangs in gray tangles from their tops, giving them the appearance of gray-haired elders gathered in the water. My friend Yasmin and I steer our kayak among them, following our guide in his single kayak ahead. Our friends and fellow adventurers, Celeste and Amy, are close behind.

Threading a path between the swelling trunks, we make our way quietly, like strangers who have stumbled into a gathering to which we have not been invited. The water is a mirror. Our kayaks skate the surface, sending ripples of widening circles into the endless reflections all around.

It is autumn in George L. Smith State Park.

The park, in southeast Georgia's Emanuel County, holds a manmade lake, with trails on land and water, beautiful in all seasons. But in autumn the park stages a grand finale, the foliage of the cypress trees flaming into gold. We have timed our November visit accordingly. Our guide, Wesley, leads us among the shadowy trunks, and we are rewarded with gold leaves flickering everywhere in the light of the lowering sun, images offered to us again in the reflections below. We drift slowly, reluctant to disturb the water with our paddles. The tiniest ripple sets the reflections to shimmering.

OPPOSITE: *The dark tannins in the water of the lake at George L. Smith State Park make the water a mirror. The late afternoon light in the foliage is captured here with watercolor washes, into which I dropped salt to create the dappled pattern of sunlight sifting through the fiery leaves. The small figure of the kayaker shows the scale of the massive cypress trunks.*

The cypress groves of George L. Smith State Park light the shoreline each November. For this scene, the focus is on the waterline, so the viewer can experience what we did—losing ourselves in the glowing foliage and the deep shadows beneath.

Amy and Celeste chat with Wesley. He shares that he left his corporate job several years ago to run this kayak service full time, guiding visitors through the water trails of the park year-round. He turns from us now and urges us forward, saying the best show is at sunset on the open lake. We quicken our strokes as he takes us out of the trees and into open water.

Bursting like a golden fire in a sea of blue, a grove of cypress glows before us between sky and water, its reflection magnified in the depths below. It hovers over the lake like some celestial apparition. We put our paddles aside. Silently, we allow ourselves to drift, marveling at this strange unearthly sight.

We have no words to match this beauty. We can only look in wonder.

After long minutes, Wesley quietly finishes the tour, taking us to the end of the kayak trail, where a covered bridge spans the dam that created the lake. He finishes with a ghost story as the trees fall into darkness. We leave for our night's lodging, for dinner, and to savor the day's memories at our bed-and-breakfast. Our cup is full.

—A. L.

In 1975 the State of Georgia purchased about fourteen hundred acres of gently rolling pineland in Emanuel County to protect a historic gristmill, covered bridge, and scenic lake and its surroundings. Five years later, the site became a state park through the efforts of local citizens. At their urging, the state named it for one of Emanuel County's most beloved natives, George L. Smith, a former speaker of the Georgia House of Representatives who pushed for the park before he died in 1973.

His legacy, the George L. Smith State Park, is now a jewel of the state's park system. The old water-powered mill and its covered bridge, built in 1880 by a James M. Parrish, sit at the edge of the park's peaceful, 412-acre lake—the pond that powered the old mill. Towering tupelo and cypress trees dot the lake, creating picture-perfect reflections in the mirror-smooth water. The setting is one of the most breathtakingly beautiful scenes in Georgia, say artists and photographers who frequent the park.

But when the park was created in the 1970s, its backers may not have realized that they were preserving more than just history. Over the years, George L. Smith State Park has also gained recognition as an exceptional natural area. Geologists, biologists, and naturalists have identified several different habitats in the park—sand hills, bay swamps, hardwood swamps, and others. Some of those habitats, especially the sand hills, harbor some of Georgia's rarest plant and animal species. Today visitors come to the park not only for its history and serenity but for its natural treasures as well.

The remarkably picturesque lake is the park's centerpiece. It was created by damming Fifteen Mile Creek, which runs through the park, to power Parrish's mill operations—first a saw mill, then a cotton gin, and finally a gristmill. The dam, built by hand at the greatest depth of water in the creek, was considered an engineering feat in its day. Situated at the dam, the mill and covered bridge actually were combined, perhaps the only such structure in the nation. The road to the mill passed over the dam, through the mill, and out the other side.

Though the lake—or pond, as locals call it—was artificial, its natural beauty today is spellbinding. It beckons one to get into a canoe and paddle among the thick stands of bald cypress, pond cypress, and water tupelo trees draped in Spanish moss. Along the way, paddlers are likely to see beavers, blue herons, great egrets, white ibises, and other colorful wading birds—and perhaps an alligator. Songbirds sing and flit about in the trees and shrubs lining the shore—a reason birdwatchers call the park a birding hotspot.

One of the most interesting trees growing along the lake is the Ogeechee lime, also known as the Ogeechee tupelo. George L. Smith Park is one of the northernmost points of its natural range, which mostly is in Florida; the park is perhaps the best place to see the tree in Georgia. A deciduous tree growing fifty feet or more, its attractive, red, edible fruits often float in clusters in the water. The fruits' tart juice once was a substitute for lime juice. The tree's name derives from Georgia's Ogeechee River, where it was first discovered by William Bartram. Honeybees make a delicious honey, the famed tupelo honey, from the nectar of its flowers. In autumn, Ogeechee limes sport a brilliant display of colorful foliage ranging from vivid yellow to deep purple.

But equally nice autumn colors come from the trees standing tall in the lake—the cypresses and tupelos. Around mid-November the cypresses' needle-like leaves transition from green to a brilliant orangish-copper hue. Their reflections in the lake's water around that time are stunning, whether seen from a boat or the land. Adding striking reddish-yellow tinges to the palette are the autumn-tinted leaves of water tupelos. Leaf peepers make special trips to the park in late autumn just to see the fall colors.

The park has another outstanding ecosystem—a large swath of upland sand hills with deep white sandy soil. South Georgia has an extensive network of these dry, sparsely vegetated habitats. Much of South Georgia was covered by the ocean millions of years ago, and sandy deposits from that period were exposed as the sea receded. Wind and water have reworked these deposits, resulting in sand hill environments like those at George L. Smith State Park. Despite their dryness and somewhat desolate appearance, sand hills are biologically diverse, home to many rare species of wild animals and plants. Botanists have found more than 180 species of native plants there, some of which grow only on sand hills. The park is considered a notable example of such an environment, which visitors can see from a winding trail. Many visitors find a special kind of beauty in the sand hills.

The sand hills also are home to a sizeable population of one of Georgia's iconic creatures, the gopher tortoise, the state's official reptile. The shy animal is the Southeast's only land tortoise species. It forages on low-growing plants and digs its burrow deep in the sand hills' loose soils. More than 250 other species—including frogs, lizards, snakes, mice, skunks, foxes, and beetles—also may rely on tortoise burrows for shelter and nesting places. Thus the gopher tortoise is called a keystone species because so many other animals depend on it.

The gopher tortoise itself, however, is in serious decline. Habitat destruction from development, logging, agriculture, and other problems has greatly reduced its populations. That's why protected areas like George L. Smith State Park have become vitally important in safeguarding Georgia's natural heritage.

—C. S.

18 Flint River and Sprewell Bluff

Pristine river offers views of rocky cliffs, rare white lilies

We were getting close to the river. I knew this because approaching us on the roadside was a young man with an armful of long-stemmed white flowers—the white spider lilies that bloom by the thousands on the Flint River each spring.

I slowed my truck and rolled down the window.

"You're really not supposed to pick those flowers," I said. "They're endangered."

"They are?" He looked startled or at least gave a good imitation of it.

We continued to bump down the gravel road to a small muddy boat launch next to Big Lazer Creek. The Flint River, which begins south of Atlanta and flows into Florida, was supposedly just downstream. With me in the truck were my friend Yasmin and a recruit, her buddy Emily, an outdoors enthusiast and—more important—the only one of us who actually knew much about handling kayaks, three of which were stacked in a sandwich on the back of my truck.

Under Emily's supervision, we unloaded the kayaks. As I untied the straps, I was tingling with anticipation and nervousness—what would we see?

We had come to the Flint River for the blooming of the rocky shoals spider lilies. Each spring these rare flowers light the river with glowing white coronas and great curving rays of petals, the blossoms rising three feet above the water. The lilies grow in the unspoiled rocky shoals of only a few rivers in the Southeast—in Georgia, the Savannah, Chattahoochee, and Flint Rivers.

Swift waters, shallow and rocky, are the shoal lilies' only habitat. The rocks provide a foothold for new bulbs; fast-flowing, oxygen-rich water nourishes the roots; and the shallows allow the plants to grow in the sun and beckon their natural pollinators—primarily moths, which arrive late in the day and stay into the night.

The naturalist William Bartram first encountered the lilies in 1773 in his explorations of Georgia, on "the cataracts of Augusta" on the Savannah River. He noted the pleasant odiferous scent of the flowers as they opened just before sunset and surmised correctly that their smell attracted their evening pollinators. The green colonies of lilies become fields of white stars on the water when they bloom, which happens each spring from mid-May through June.

Ever since reading Bartram's account, I'd dreamed of seeing the lilies in person.

The Flint River is one of the few rivers in the country that flows unimpeded and protected for two hundred miles—in the Flint's case, almost 220. Its clear waters harbor mussels, fish, and other species found nowhere else—entities with unlikely names like Halloween darter and shiny-rayed pocketbook mussel.

And the rocky shoals spider lily.

Number 18 on Charlie Seabrook's bucket list was Sprewell Bluff Park. I had managed to translate this into "Flint River" and, naturally, an excuse to finally see Bartram's shoal lilies in bloom.

OPPOSITE: *Twilight makes a shimmering world of light and shadow on the Flint River. Across the water, darkness pools under the trees, while their crowns still glow in the day's last light. The lilies are also cast into shadow, but, growing in the open shallows, they gather the reflected light from the sky and appear to glow from within.*

The ever-knowledgeable Hal Massie of the Georgia Botanical Society was happy to share with me directions to an obscure launch near the lilies. We nudged our kayaks into the creek and paddled hopefully downstream toward the Flint, which was just a couple hundred yards away.

The sun was riding low in the sky as we approached the confluence of the creek and river. There, in the widening shallows of the Flint, the lilies spread in bright green islands, raising tall white flowers among the rocks in an offering to the sky. It was an unearthly garden, magically growing in the middle of a river.

We could hardly believe what we were seeing. Tentatively, we paddled our kayaks into the shallows and began to look, photograph, and exclaim.

The lilies spangled the rippling fields of green in great multitudes, white stars with rays of petals shooting out from the corona like the beams of small suns. *Spider* didn't fit these blossoms or do them justice. The sunset light traced delicate blue shadows across the wide white trumpets of the corona, and the interiors glowed pale green, releasing their sweet perfume in a fragrant cloud across the water.

We abandoned our kayaks on the rocky shoals and waded carefully, joyously, into the clear shallows among the lilies. We exclaimed again and again, in a kind of daze, "This is incredible." "Where *is* this?!" "Why have I never heard of this place?!"

The sun sank and the clear blue river and pink sky merged. The trees on the banks faded into shadows. The sweet scent of the blossoms called to the winged pollinators as the sun set—bees and flies, a swallowtail. Sometime in the night, perhaps, the sphinx moths (also called hawk moths) would arrive.

Bartram saw something like this more than two centuries ago. Seldom are you permitted to encounter something of such great unspoiled beauty. A dream from the past, still living.

—A. L.

Watercolor washes are glazed in layers to create the luminous colors of sunset. I rendered the tallest lily almost translucent, the river landscape visible through its beautiful but transitory flowering.

Writers, poets, environmentalists, and veteran river travelers have long praised the beauty of Georgia's Flint River. "The Flint is arguably Georgia's most beautiful river, and in terms of the terrain through which it flows on its 344-mile journey, there is not another Georgia river that exposes the river traveler to more diverse vistas," says the veteran environmentalist Joe Cook in his authoritative book *Flint River User's Guide*.

Despite its superb beauty, the Flint has a humble, squalid beginning just south of Atlanta—as a groundwater seep emanating from fractured crystalline rocks beneath the runways at Hartsfield-Jackson International Airport, the world's busiest airport. But from there, the river amazingly transforms into its natural splendor as it flows to the Florida line and joins the Chattahoochee River to form the Apalachicola River. The Apalachicola then flows across the Florida Panhandle to the Gulf of Mexico.

Despite the three dams in its lower section, the upper portion of the Flint still claims its place among only forty rivers in the contiguous forty-eight states with free-flowing, unimpeded stretches of two hundred miles or more. That long run helps make the Flint one of the cleanest, most naturally beautiful, and ecologically diverse streams in Georgia.

A variety of habitats—swamps, stands of montane longleaf pine, hardwood forested slopes—line its shores for the Flint's entire length, and they teem with an amazing assortment of plant and animal life. The river itself is home to about eighty-five fish species, including the shoal bass, a prized sport fish that attracts anglers from across Georgia and around the nation. The river also hosts more than twenty freshwater mussel species; their presence in a stream indicates good water quality.

As the river winds across the western side of Georgia, geologists, biologists, and others divide it into three distinct sections—upper, middle, and lower—based on landscape, channel characteristics, and flora and fauna.

The upper Flint lies solely within the rolling Piedmont region, flowing mostly through a deeply incised channel etched into crystalline rocks that form stunning cliffs, ravines, and other remarkable geological features—especially at a stretch called Sprewell Bluff. The upper Flint's striking beauty drew the praise of the now-defunct Georgia Natural Areas Council, which said in a 1970 report on Georgia

Rivers: "The upper portion of the Flint is undoubtedly the most picturesque stream in the Georgia Piedmont."

As it nears the fall line in Middle Georgia, the river changes into raging whitewater rapids, the most famous of which is the rock-strewn Yellow Jacket Shoals. Within a mile stretch, the river drops about forty feet through the shoals, creating challenges for boaters but also providing habitat for the shoal bass and one of Georgia's most beautiful and rare wildflowers, the shoals spider lily. Here is where Spanish moss first appears along the river, probably the only place in Georgia where Spanish moss, an epiphyte common to the coastal plain, overlooks a Class III rapid.

As the river spills over the fall line into the coastal plain, the middle Flint transforms into a broad, forested, swampy flood plain partly occupied by the so-called Great Swamp. The swamp helps clean the river water, provides nutrients to the river, and serves as habitat for numerous species of reptiles, amphibians, mammals, and songbirds—including the prothonotary warbler, one of the South's most colorful birds. The Montezuma Bluffs Nature Area, also along this river segment, protects one of Georgia's largest populations of the rare relict trillium, a plant in the lily family that has dark purple to yellow flowers.

South of Lake Blackshear in South Georgia, the lower Flint flows through a channel in limestone rock above the Floridan Aquifer, the great underground reservoir that provides water for much of southwestern Georgia and northwestern Florida. Groundwater seeping from the aquifer's deep limestone caverns through numerous blue hole springs helps maintain the Flint's flow.

No major dams impede the Flint until it reaches Lake Blackshear on its lower section. The Warwick Dam impounds the lower Flint to create the eighty-seven-hundred-acre lake that borders five South Georgia counties. Downstream from there, two other dams create reservoirs on the river.

But if there is one "must-see" place to view the Flint in all its glory, it is a place on the upper Flint called Sprewell Bluff in Upson County. Here, a four-mile stretch of the river cuts through the eastern end of Pine Mountain (see chapter 10) and carves breathtaking gorges with cliffs and bluffs several hundred feet above the river's course. About two hundred acres of Sprewell Bluff are managed as a park by Upson County, but the rest of the surrounding area is Sprewell Bluff Wildlife Management Area. The beauty and biological diversity of Sprewell Bluff can hardly be overstated: it is a true botanical melting pot that is home to mountain, Piedmont, and coastal plain flora and fauna. For instance, dwarf palmetto, common on the coastal plain, can be found only a few feet from trees and shrubs more common in the Appalachian Mountains.

But in the 1970s, Sprewell Bluff—and all surrounding it—came close to being inundated by a lake from a dam that the U.S. Army Corps of Engineers wanted to build there. Jimmy Carter, then Georgia's governor, saved Sprewell Bluff from that fate. Carter persistently raised strong legitimate questions about the true long-term benefits of the dam and finally vetoed the project. Even so, talk of building a dam at Sprewell Bluff has never gone away, and conservationists, river enthusiasts, nature lovers, and their allies remain vigilant.

—C. S.

19 The Palisades on the Chattahoochee River

A river wilderness in the heart of the city

I drove the octopus arm of Interstate 75 as it curled into Atlanta's sprawling perimeter highway. I was on my way to meet one of Charlie Seabrook's wonders. I felt, as always, a flutter of anticipation. But this time it was tinged with mystery: I was headed for a natural wonder in a city.

The Palisades of the Chattahoochee River are enfolded by some of the most exclusive neighborhoods in Atlanta—Buckhead and Sandy Springs, not far from the gleaming towers of the Cumberland-Galleria area. The Palisades are cliffs, steep rock walls that jut up from the banks of the Chattahoochee River. They were named for the famous Palisades cliffs that begin in northern New Jersey and run north along the Hudson River for nearly twenty miles.

My map showed the ribbon of Interstate 75 crossing the Chattahoochee. I had driven past this area thousands of times. Like many Atlantans, I'd even floated past it—"shootin' the Hooch" on an inner tube, drinking wine coolers one lazy afternoon in my long-ago twenties.

What wonder had I missed in the heart of the metropolis?

Quiet neighborhoods and wooded hills ushered me into the parking lot for the East Palisades Trail. From the trailhead, the path crossed a footbridge

and then followed the eastern bank of the river. On this early weekday morning, a morning jogger was the only other person I saw.

The river shimmered in the early morning light. I stood on the eastern bank, still cast in shadow, and peered between the dark bars of trees. Across the water, spring cast over the hills a soft rainbow of color, the myriad greens and golds and pinks of new leaves.

The river's waters had ebbed through the winter, exposing gleaming arrays of flat rocks. They spread across the shallows like steppingstones for giants. One set tipped upward, levered from its resting place by some mighty thrust of the earth.

I marveled. Looking across the river in that misty light, I saw no signs that this wilderness held at bay the surging growth of one of the largest metropolitan areas in the South.

Now the trail began to climb. I clambered up rocky ledges to meet the Palisades, grasping for handholds where the ground became slippery.

Flowers appeared along the path, spring dangling its baubles like a magician pulling tricks from a hat: trembling white Carolina silverbell, azalea blushing deep pink, mountain laurel with its intricate pentagons, the starry reds of fire pink (*Silene virginica L.*), and leucothoe with its clusters of white.

As I climbed among the twisted trees and lichen-covered rocks, the mystery of this urban wild deepened. I couldn't help but think of magic places, like Narnia or maybe Hogwarts, destinations reached by spells or wizardry. Where was I?

At last I came out of the trees to a wooden observation deck perched on the edge of the cliff. From here I could see the blue tapestry of the Chattahoochee below, streaked with stones gleaming in shining rows—the

The blossoms of Carolina silverbell dangle from the boughs of the small flowering tree. The leaf at top of the painting captures the temperature range of the sun's light as it plays across foliage: pale and cool where it glints on the leaf directly and a glowing golden green where it shines through the transparent underside.

OPPOSITE: *The morning sun breached the high hills along the Chattahoochee River, illuminating the soft pinks and golds of new foliage and blazing the pines on the river island with light. Here I delineated the rocks in the water with line alone, not color, so that the brilliant blue of the river remains unbroken.*

Devil's Race Course, I recalled, so named by the boatmen who navigated the river in the nineteenth century.

Now, a few kayaks were the only sign of watercraft. From this high point I finally saw signs of the city—one or two structures peeping from the trees just north across the river, and on the northwest horizon, the skyscrapers of Cumberland and Galleria.

But across the river I could see only a wall of bright trees climbing the hills in a magical bubble of wilderness within a city—perhaps larger on the inside than it appeared from the outside.

I walked a wide loop on my return, visiting the famous bamboo forest, circling the high hills in the morning sun, listening to the birds. I knew that the houses of Buckhead were close yet invisible.

Leaving the park, I took a final look across the river. Out on the water a half-dozen cormorants preened and sunned on a rock, their wings outstretched.

The Palisades no longer seemed a mystery but still perhaps a bit of magic.

—A. L.

I returned to the Palisades in the fall and found this rare second blooming of a native rhododendron. In this work I sought to re-create what seemed to me a masterful tapestry of foliage and flowers at the hand of nature: an ecstatic weaving of weighted waxy leaves and vivid translucent blossoms.

Indigo-tinted ink creates the shadowy trunk of the huge oak leaning from the slopes of the Palisades. Just beyond glows the foliage of smaller trees lit in the morning sun, with a glimpse on the high distant horizon of the Galleria's towers—the only hint of the Palisades' urban location .

With steep rugged cliffs, scenic rocky shoals, and spectacularly high bluffs, the Palisades section of the Chattahoochee River in metro Atlanta is one of the most awe-inspiring places along the river's entire 430 miles. This section also is remarkable for another reason: it forms a breathtaking view of nature amid one of the nation's biggest, busiest, and fastest-growing urban areas.

The Palisades is one of fifteen parks along the river that make up the majestic fifty-two-hundred-acre Chattahoochee River National Recreation Area (CRNRA), a national park. Like a necklace of sparkling emeralds, the parks stretch forty-eight miles along the river, from Buford Dam on Lake Lanier to the river's confluence with Peachtree Creek inside Atlanta's city limits. The river's course follows a remarkable geologic feature, the Brevard Fault, one of North America's oldest and most stable river channels. It is responsible for the national park's stunning ridges, cliffs, and rock faces, including those in the Palisades.

Because of its exceptional natural splendor, the Palisades is often touted as the most scenic section of the CRNRA. It begins about a half-mile downstream from where I-285 crosses the river, making it the southernmost stretch of the recreation area. The Chattahoochee actually splits the Palisades into two park units—East Palisades and West Palisades, which are on opposite sides of the river from one another.

As it flows between the two units, the river speeds up and rushes through turbulent—yet picturesque—rocky shoals. This is the famed stretch known as the Devil's Race Course, so named by river boatmen in the late 1800s because the shoals were a devil to navigate. Even today the stretch can be challenging to boaters. Kayakers and canoeists regularly come here to practice their paddling skills in the whitewater strewn with boulders. Anglers come here, too: the cold water spewing out of Buford Dam upstream makes the Chattahoochee pleasing to rainbow and brown trout as far as the Palisades—the nation's southernmost habitat for the highly prized fish, which require cool water for survival.

On each side of the Palisades, broken cliffs of especially hard quartzite rock, four hundred million years old, rise abruptly along the river in a gorge-like setting. Both sides feature fertile forested floodplains, ridges, and ravines. During the early 1900s the steep terrains made logging difficult on both sides, and their dense hardwood forests remained mostly untouched.

Today the rich forests muffle city noises. About the only sounds are singing birds, buzzing insects, and rushing water as the river swirls and eddies among the jumble of rocks. It could be a scene from an unspoiled wilderness in North Georgia's mountains.

The 303-acre East Palisades park harbors one of the river's most impressive and well-known natural features—the so-called Diving Rock. Jutting out like a huge shelf over the river, it is a massive boulder lodged about twenty-five feet over the water. Countless Atlantans over several generations have daringly plunged from the Diving Rock into the cool green river water below, which is fifteen feet deep there. In 1972, when he was Georgia's governor, Jimmy Carter took the plunge to call attention to preservationists' efforts to save the Palisades from development.

A splendid 3.4-mile loop trail, sometimes known as the Overlook Trail, winds through the East Palisades. It takes hikers along the river past some historic ruins, through a resplendent bamboo forest with thirty-foot stalks (originally planted by settlers), and then up the steep bluff to a wooden observation deck 160 feet above the river. The platform offers spectacular views of the Devil's Race Course and the Brevard Fault. In its entirety, the 320-mile fault forms the dividing line between the Appalachian Mountains and the Piedmont Plateau.

In the 302-acre West Palisades are some of metro Atlanta's most majestic oaks, tulip poplars, and hickories, many of which are more than two feet in diameter. The forest, park rangers say, is probably like the one that Native Americans were used to, before Europeans arrived. Now, it helps clean the air and water of a big city and refreshes the weary minds of its people. In late winter, the West Palisades becomes a mecca of sorts for wildflower lovers, who come to see one of Georgia's earliest-blooming native plants, the trout lily. Beginning in mid-February, thousands of blooming yellow-flowered trout lilies cover the wooded hillsides along Rottenwood Creek in the West Palisades, a superb scene. As the year progresses, numerous other wildflowers come into bloom according to the seasons.

For history buffs, the Palisades and the rest of the CRNRA can be a bonanza. Humans may have been living in the national park's river corridor as long as twelve thousand years ago. In the eighteenth century, the river was a border between the Cherokee and Creek Indian nations. Today archaeological sites within the CRNRA include forty-seven Native American villages, campsites, and hamlets and sixteen rock overhangs where prehistoric inhabitants sought shelter and camped. One of the most impressive of these so-called rock caves can be found in the East Palisades.

Europeans and their enslaved Africans established farms and built cotton mills and gristmills and other factories along the river and its tributaries to take advantage of hydropower. The stark remains of some mills still stand in the CRNRA. Among them are the ruins of the old Akers Mill, a complex of at least two late nineteenth-century gristmills along Rottenwood Creek in the West Palisades.

The story of how the river became protected and the CRNRA was created is remarkable. In the early 1970s, the Palisades and the fourteen other parks were in danger of succumbing to development and pollution. Against what seemed overwhelming odds, a group of foresighted residents who called themselves the River Rats—with help from Junior League members and visionary government leaders—worked tirelessly to save and safeguard the river and its magnificent banks. Spurring the River Rats to action was the almost accidental discovery of plans for a pair of huge sewer lines along the Palisades. The residents were able to stop the pipes. Then they came up with an even bolder plan—a national park from Buford Dam all the way down to Peachtree Creek.

On August 15, 1978, President Jimmy Carter signed the bill that Congress had just passed to create the CRNRA. Congress authorized its boundaries to encompass ten thousand acres, even though the federal government has acquired only about half that amount for the park. Even so, for Atlanta today, the CRNRA has become a priceless natural sanctuary, one of the nation's premier urban parks where visitors can enjoy a near-wilderness experience. Because of its rich assortment of flora and fauna, the CRNRA is also one of the nation's most biologically diverse national parks. As Carter said when he signed the CRNRA bill: "It's a rare occasion when within the city limits of one of our major cities, one can find pure water and trout and free canoeing and rapids and the seclusion of the Earth the way God made it. But the Chattahoochee River is this kind of place."

—C. S.

20 Graves Mountain

Treasure trove of rocks and minerals for collectors from around the world

More than a hundred people stood outside the metal gate that guards Graves Mountain, a geological wonder that attracts rock collectors from all over the world.

Yasmin and I listened to the swirl of excited chatter and eyed the chisels and hammers poking from packs and tool belts in this friendly invasion force. Accompanying many were hand trucks or rolling coolers—although the October morning was cool, refreshments would no doubt be welcome later in the day.

A voice from the front carried above the crowd, “We’re just waitin’ for Junior to open the gate.”

We’d arrived for the semiannual Graves Mountain public dig, an event that draws hundreds of rock enthusiasts each spring and fall. They come to this obscure mountain in East Georgia’s Lincoln County for the dazzling rocks and minerals embedded in it—specimens of a variety and quantity rivaling any collection site in the world. Here the remains of ancient ocean volcanoes a half-billion years old melted and were molded into a metamorphic treasure trove, entities with exotic names like lazulite, pyrite, iridescent hematite. Once upon a time, the mountain was an active mining site, its products used in industrial processes ranging from polishing diamonds

to insulating spark plugs. Now a multinational conglomerate, Asea Brown Boveri ABB, owns the mountain and oversees ongoing remediation mandated for chemical runoff. The site has a caretaker who arranges access for visiting groups and researchers, as well as organizing the public digs.

The gate swung open.

Yasmin and I were swept through the entrance in a human river: grizzled old men, middle-aged couples, a few young families with kids loaded in pull carts. One dog of dubious parentage wore a hand-lettered sign that hung rakishly about his neck: ROCK HOUND, it said. There was a general carnival atmosphere. It reminded me of the county fairs of my childhood, when each summer, half the town lined up at the fairground for opening day.

The website announcement of the public dig—all caps in large font centered on the page—was the first clue to the hometown spirit of this event:

THESE DIGS ARE OPEN TO ALL
NO NEED TO SIGN-UP, JUST SHOW UP FOR ALL "ROCK SWAP AND DIGS"!

Yasmin and I walked past the rows of tables just inside the gate. Standing beneath a nearby canopy was "Junior" himself—Clarence Norman Jr., caretaker of the site. Surrounding him at the table were his family members—a smiling wife, daughter, and two sons standing tall and proud. Something about their friendly faces and their slight country accents conjured a wholesome picture of Americana and apple pie. Yasmin chatted with them in her easygoing way, and we asked to take their picture.

Friendly vendors presided over tables groaning with rocks. Placards proclaimed, WILL SELL OR SWAP. Rock specimens dazzled with glittering facets, startling hues, or fantastic forms that beckoned all passersby. Yasmin and I found ourselves beguiled and then held captive, helpless under the spell of the dizzying beauty and variety. The rocks were iridescent with

The caretaker of Graves Mountain, Clarence "Junior" Norman, far right, with his family.

OPPOSITE: *The rocks of Graves Mountain form an alien landscape of rose, lilac, copper, and chartreuse, their colors recombining in the swirling pools below. Two small figures at the bottom left pull a wagon with cooler and tools along the road. They lend a sense of scale to this otherwise unearthly scene.*

blues and reds and golds or sprouting with cauliflower-like forms or flashing arrays of glassy crystals. Their names were fantastical—such as ilmenite, fuchsite, woodhouseite, and crandallite. I felt myself succumbing to a sudden fever, an obsession to find and hoard. As we held up one sample after another, we exclaimed our admiration and awe.

Finally, we pulled ourselves away and entered the main pit. A woman stationed there answered questions, enthusiastically directing us to the ridge two hundred feet above us for the best bird's-eye view.

The main pit yawned wide, a gaping crater of rose-colored rock that looked like something from another planet, a set dreamed up perhaps for a *Star Wars* sequel. Slashes of lilac, gold, and orange streaked the cliffs surrounding the pit, their hues reflected in the holding pool below. Tinted a deep rose at the edges, the water, I learned later, owes its color to iron compounds leached from pyrite in the rock walls.

We watched the activity across the floor of the pit as collectors made their way to crevices or rock walls to set up their dig for the day. Turning away from the pit, Yasmin and I began trudging up the road to the overlook.

A strapping young man drove up in an ATV to offer us a ride. Yasmin asked if this was his job. He smiled and said with visible pride, no, he was a volunteer like everyone else here. If volunteers didn't show up to open the mountain for the digs in April and October, he told us, no one would have access to this place at all.

We declined his offer—we wanted to hike up ourselves. As we approached the summit, a sign warned us away from the edge: A FALL ENDANGERS NOT JUST YOURSELF, BUT THOSE BELOW.

From the top, the view of the main pit was a rainbow moonscape of bright reds, pale greens, golds, pinks, and gray-blues splashed on the exposed cliff walls. Eons of rock merged in a maelstrom of color. The holding pool was a mirror rimmed in deep orange red. Mesmerized, we took scores of photos, as I tried vainly to lock the colors into my memory.

We left the overlook to explore the rocky outcrops at the top, more walls of orange and lilac and even chartreuse rising beside smaller pools of acid water tinted the pervasive red and orange.

When we returned to the main pit, the sun was at its zenith. The crowd had doubled. Everywhere were dogs with bandannas, children with sunhats, adults sipping drinks in beach chairs while their more motivated family members toiled nearby. The last were easy to spot—heads down, chipping steadily with chisels and picks. Their hand carts brimmed with specimens. Some scaled the high walls to dig on narrow ledges, their small forms silhouetted against the pale cliffs of pink, rose, and peach.

Yasmin and I spoke to one last table vendor before we left. He showed us samples of the mountain's famous rutile, its beautiful steel-gray crystals mined in the 1920s by Tiffany & Co. to cut diamonds. A good-sized sample was expensive, well more than $1,000.

We left that afternoon, perhaps the only visitors not weighted with pounds of rock. The fever had subsided, and I departed feeling light, unburdened by my treasures (photos). But I carried with me the shining weightless memories of this beautiful Georgia natural wonder. Graves Mountain had revealed its rarest and most marvelous find—a local community, opening to share its wealth with the world.

—A. L.

Among rockhounds, Graves Mountain is world-famous, an international mecca for collecting a variety of treasured rocks and minerals. Professional collectors from all over the country as well as local families with kids in tow come here twice a year in hope of finding a rare valuable crystal—or just some pretty rocks to take home. For many children, digging at Graves Mountain has inspired a lifelong interest in geology.

The Georgia Mineral Society calls Graves Mountain a "unique geological formation." The mountain itself is an isolated twin-peaked monadnock (a dramatic dome-like formation) with a saddle between the peaks. After decades of commercial strip mining and collecting by countless rock hunters, the peaks today are less than half their original height of five hundred feet—mostly what remains are two massive pits left over from the mining. Though the mining has ceased, the pits still yield highly desirable rocks and minerals for collectors and anyone else willing to dig in the dirt.

According to geologists, the rock of Graves Mountain began about 560 million years ago as ash from a volcanic island chain in the proto-Atlantic Ocean. Continental collisions, part of the geologic process known as continental drift, then forced the volcanic remains into the Earth's mantle. Hot mineral-rich fluids altered the ash, which then, under tremendous heat and pressure, became the other rocks and minerals that make up Graves Mountain today.

About fifty different types of minerals may be found here—such as barite, blue quartz and quartz crystals, kyanite, muscovite, pyrophyllite, and others. But one mineral in particular, rutile (titanium oxide), made Graves Mountain world-famous. Rutile forms brilliant red to reddish brown metallic crystals, the finer specimens of which may command thousands of dollars. Some choice rutile specimens are cut into gems.

Graves Mountain became famous in 1859 after scientific journals described it as a place where some of the planet's finest and largest specimens of rutile were lying on or just under the ground. Infatuated by the reports, rockhounds started coming from as far away as Germany to collect the lustrous crystals.

Demand for Graves Mountain rutile increased. In the early 1920s, when Tiffany & Co. began mining rutile at Graves Mountain, it used lower grades of rutile for diamond polishing but also helped meet the demand for high-quality rutile. Today many of the finer rutile specimens from the mountain are on display in museums around the world, including the Smithsonian Museum of Natural History in Washington, D.C.

In addition to rutile, Tiffany's also mined from Graves Mountain another lustrous mineral that is highly sought after, lazulite. But in the 1930s, geologists discovered that Graves Mountain was top heavy in a lucrative mineral called kyanite, which had become valuable in industry. Kyanite, which typically has a bluish color, has a high melting point and maintains its strength at exceedingly high temperatures. Those properties make it ideal for use in a variety of heat-resistant products, including spark plugs, porcelain plumbing, and electrical insulators. Kyanite also has had a role in space—it was used for making Space Shuttle tiles to protect the spacecraft from the tremendous heat of reentry.

To meet the demand for kyanite, Combustion Chemicals purchased Graves Mountain in the mid-1960s to strip-mine for the mineral. The firm, a subsidiary of Combustion Engineering, conducted mining operations there until 1984, when the property was sold to Pasco Mining. Pasco mined it until November 1986, at which time the property and all environmental responsibilities reverted to Combustion Chemicals under a previous agreement. Combustion Chemicals halted mining there because of environmental concerns.

In 1990 Combustion Engineering became a subsidiary of ABB, one of the largest electrical engineering companies in the world. The next year, sixteen property owners surrounding the mountain sued Combustion Engineering because acid runoff from the mining, they said, was damaging their properties. ABB and its subsidiary paid to remediate the environmental damage and permanently ended kyanite mining there.

Despite the mining, the mountain is still studied for the unique scientific and geologic wonder that it is. Ironically, the mining was a boon to rock collectors: the mining created two gaping pits that exposed a multitude of desirable minerals accessible to collectors. Thanks to the efforts of mineral societies in Georgia, the generosity of ABB, which still owns the mountain, and the property's caretakers, Graves Mountain is now open to the public two weekends each year—in April and October. Those who want to dig there or just see the place are asked to make a small donation.

Armed with chisels, rock hammers, picks, and other rock-mining tools, the scores of rockhounds—professional and amateur, young and old—descend into the pits to pound, scrape, and dig for the minerals. They can keep what they find. As they dig next to each other, they often swap stories about individuals who have made valuable finds over the years—such as an Augusta woman who found a huge rutile crystal worth more than $5,000. Some specimens of lazulite also have fetched thousands of dollars.

And who knows? The finest specimens of rutile or lazulite may still be awaiting discovery at Graves Mountain.

—C. S.

21 Stone, Arabia, and Panola Mountains

Geological wonders explode in colorful bloom each spring

We look across the smooth granite base of Arabia Mountain. Soft waves of flowers undulate over the hard surface, appearing to spring directly from the rock: a magic trick, some botanical feat of spontaneous generation.

It's springtime, and my sisters Jane and Julie have joined me for a visit to Davidson-Arabia Mountain Nature Preserve in the Piedmont east of Atlanta. Both are avid hikers—between them, they have trekked the length of the Western Hemisphere, from Alaska's Denali to the South American Andes.

But I'm hopeful they've never seen anything like Arabia Mountain in April.

Arabia Mountain is a monadnock, a granite outcrop similar to nearby Stone Mountain. But unlike its more famous cousin, Arabia is wild and undeveloped. When we arrive at the trailhead, we're greeted by a bare landscape of rock: it's apparent no skyride or railroad will detract from our hike through this spring garden.

A sign at the trailhead explains the mystery of Arabia's flowers: key are the shallow depressions on the exposed granitic gneiss. After a rainfall, each depression becomes a fleeting oasis, providing water for seeds to sprout and take root. Across millennia a hardy community of plant adventurers has thus gained a foothold on the mountain, slowly eroding the shallow basins and adding each year to the thin layer of gravel and organic matter.

Arabia's most famous resident is a tiny plant called red elf orpine. This succulent is the first plant to colonize the shallow rock hollows, storing enough water in its miniscule leaves to sustain it through a dry spell. Its seed sprouts in winter, growing a rosette of red leaves, followed by white flowers in spring; these produce the next year's seeds. A fragile threadlike stem holds each seed aloft, protecting it from summer's scorching heat: temperatures on the rock can reach 120 degrees Fahrenheit—fatal to any seed that falls or is crushed by a passing footstep.

We follow the stone pillars that mark the trail. We step carefully around the gravel spots.

Elf orpine sweeps the base of the mountain in extravagant red curves just an inch or two high. Jane and Julie exclaim at the fiery carpet; they compare it with the landscape of a fall hike they shared in the Allegheny Mountains—a craggy peak called Dolly Sods, which they describe as covered with acres of blazing red blueberry bushes. The picture hovers, vivid in my mind's eye.

I feel a pang of envy. Once upon a time, Jane and I did everything together—we ignored the two baby sisters, Julie and Liza. "The little ones," we called them. Now we four are well into our fifties. Liza lives close to me but doesn't enjoy the outdoors as I do. Julie and Jane, however, are separated by only a three-hour drive—close enough to hike together on weekends. So I am the odd one out.

Yet Jane and Julie's description of Dolly Sods, its peak cloaked in brilliant red, somehow fills me with pleasure. The picture seems to trickle into this shared experience on Arabia, coloring and connecting it with the memory of another natural wonder from a different place and time.

We reach the top. Arabia's peak is a moonscape high above the Piedmont. Adorning its rolling summit are colorful craters—perfectly edged flower

OPPOSITE: *Dish-shaped gardens appear across the surface of Arabia Mountain, each offering a layered feast of color on the rock. Here the rising sun sets the tiers of color aglow—red elf orpine and white stonecrop, with shadowed pillows of blue lichen behind them. The reflections of the rocks in the shallow water make a sharp counterpoint to the soft masses of flowers.*

Crimson orpine washes across the surface of Arabia Mountain's rock, arriving each spring like a red tide to light the barren granite. The waves across the dark rock evoked for me the wild arc of nebulae leaping across the blackness of space, which I mimicked with salt crystals dropped into wet pigment to form a starry sweep of sky in the rock.

gardens that have grown in the shallow ovals and curves carved into the rock. The rim of each is a ring of red—the elf orpine; then, in deepening layers toward the center, the white of sandwort, the violet blue of spiderwort, and the gold of ragwort, all in bloom. A small fringe tree crowns one flowering basin with a mop of white blossoms.

My sisters and I wander across Arabia's peak, lost in the enchantment of a garden designed and tended not by humans but by nature, which is endlessly inventive.

One perfect oval of flowers pulls me close. I kneel and find myself looking into a miniature bonsai garden. A petite forest of the red orpine raises its white flowers like a flush of spring leaves in the treetops. The small branching shapes are reflected in a pool of water below that is less than a half-inch deep. A rock sits in the middle of the water, an island in an elfin land, with a twig for a bridge: this garden may live for one day before the water is gone, stolen by the sun.

Jane, Julie, and I relive our morning walk as we drive home, turning over the memories for the pleasure of seeing them again. And we begin planning new wonders to explore—traveling now not always as two but together as three.

Our sisterhood is a river flowing through time. It grows as its branches come together, collecting scattered memories and far-flung places into one stream, flowing full and wide, into the years to come.

—A. L.

The Atlanta area is home to some of the most exceptional natural habitats in the southeastern United States, the granite outcrops. They are places where bedrock—including granite and related gneiss and migmatite—lies bare at the surface, not covered by soil. A unique set of plants and animals has adapted over time to these unusual environments, creating enclaves of spectacular beauty that are among the crown jewels of Georgia's natural communities.

An estimated 90 percent of the Southeast's approximately twelve thousand acres of granite outcrops are in Georgia, and much of that is concentrated in the Atlanta area. The outcrops, according to geologists, were formed independently 300 to 375 million years ago when melted magma intruded into existing rock, cooled, and solidified—ten miles or more beneath the earth. Across great expanses of time, the land was uplifted. Erosion set in and removed thousands of feet of overlying rock and soil, exposing the more erosion-resistant bodies of granite.

Some outcrops are little more than flat rock surfaces resembling pavement and occupy only an acre or two. Others are the dramatic, dome-like formations called monadnocks that occupy hundreds of acres and rise sharply for hundreds of feet above the mostly level landscape.

In Georgia's Piedmont region, the monadnocks are called mountains. The Atlanta area has an unusual number of them, including a major group—Stone Mountain, Arabia Mountain, and Panola Mountain—within fifteen miles of one another. All three are in public parks that are magnet destinations for people eager to see the splendors of nature.

The largest and best known of Atlanta's monadnocks is the 825-foot Stone Mountain, which occupies six hundred acres in DeKalb County. From its summit, one can see Arabia and Panola Mountains to the east and southeast. The trio of monadnocks, in fact, has been called the Three Sisters because of their relative closeness and a geology that suggests they came from the same underlying rock. However, they are more like cousins that vary significantly in age, origin, and types of granite.

Stone Mountain, one of Georgia's official Seven Natural Wonders, is composed mostly of a specific type of rock called Stone Mountain granite, which formed about three hundred million years ago. Only during the past fifteen million years, however, has the mountain become exposed through erosion. Stone Mountain is world-famous for another reason—an enormous carving of Confederate Civil War leaders that occupies most of the mountain's granite face.

Arabia Mountain (172 feet), which lies within the Davidson-Arabia Mountain Nature Preserve in DeKalb County, is said to be a miniature version of Stone Mountain. However, its rock, formed about 375 million years ago, is fifty to one hundred million years older than Stone Mountain's. The rock makeup also is significantly different—a type known as Arabia Mountain gneiss, a metamorphic rock formed from granite.

Lying along the border between Henry County and Rockdale County is Panola Mountain (260 feet), which is about the age of Stone Mountain but with granite that is darker and of a different texture and mineral content. Panola granite, as the rock is known, was deemed unsuitable for industrial use—unlike the rock types at Stone Mountain and Arabia Mountain, which were heavily quarried for construction and other uses. Because it escaped quarrying, Panola is the most undisturbed monadnock in the Piedmont region. A portion of it is a protected natural area—Georgia's first conservation park—with limited public visitation. It is also a National Natural Landmark and, along with Arabia Mountain, is part of the Davidson-Arabia Mountain National Heritage Area.

But regardless of their geological differences, the monadnocks and related granite outcrops around Atlanta have many characteristics in common, which make them biological treasures as well as places of breathtaking natural beauty. This is so despite their extremely harsh conditions, including extraordinarily high water runoff—as much as 95 percent of the rain that falls on them—because of their sparse vegetation and shallow soil. Summer temperatures on rock outcrops may exceed 120 degrees Fahrenheit, creating desert-like environments within an area that, ironically, gets as much as forty-five inches of precipitation every year.

Even so, a number of rare and unusual plants and other remarkable organisms have adapted over time to the brutal environments. In particular, Atlanta's monadnocks are exceptionally rich in lichens that cover the bare rock. Mosses and other plants—and sometimes trees—grow in soil that has accumulated in cracks in the rock.

Most of the distinctive plants and animals of rock outcrops, however, are found in the numerous shallow pits that pockmark the exposed rock. Thousands of years of weathering and natural acidification by lichens carved out the pits. Some of the depressions are known as vernal pools because they temporarily fill with rainwater in winter and spring and support several rare plants, tadpoles, and an unusual crustacean species called fairy shrimp. The most colorful pits by far, however, are the so-called dish gardens where thin layers of soil have built up. Wildflowers fill the gardens in spring, but in fall endemic yellow daisies—also known as Stone Mountain daisies—create huge, strikingly beautiful swaths of bright color that contrast with other fall wildflowers.

Protecting these fragile environments has become a top goal of conservationists. Fortunately, the Atlanta area's monadnocks are now protected within public parks and preserves that are open to all who want to see nature's wonderful magic.

—C. S.

22 Tallulah Gorge

Steep cliffs frame dramatic waterfalls

Tallulah Gorge State Park, two hours northeast of Atlanta, is home to one of the deepest canyons east of the Rockies. Trails skirt the canyon rim on both sides, offering bird's-eye views of sheer granite walls and churning waterfalls hundreds of feet below.

It seemed the perfect destination for a weekend retreat.

I'm piloting my first nature journal workshop, an introduction to the basics of recording intimate experiences in nature. A nature journal can include words, drawings—even hand-drawn charts or maps—and it requires only a notebook and pen. Using a few prompts and simple techniques, anyone can discover the pleasures of nature journaling and what it's about: recovering the natural pace of life, slowing down to watch a bird, study a leaf, follow the path of an ant—that is, losing oneself in a deep experience of life and often rediscovering the curiosity and enthusiasm of childhood.

At least, that has been my experience. I hope to share it with my students. I usually journal in my backyard, so bringing the group to Tallulah Gorge was more of a bonus than a necessity. Unfortunately, this Saturday morning—the kickoff of the retreat—has dawned gray and drizzly.

We sip coffee and nibble breakfast muffins in our rented cabin just outside the park while looking out at the low-hanging clouds. I explain that

The steep cliffs of Tallulah Gorge are a theater of light and shadow, transformed hour to hour by the arc of the sun. Autumn foliage weaves a rich backdrop, while a halo of light spotlights the tall pines at the suspension bridge overlooking Hurricane Falls.

nature journaling is done in whatever conditions the moment brings. My five students—mature women all—keep up a disciplined cheerfulness. But the group is subdued as they don rain jackets and climb into the van for the short drive to the park.

If it rains any harder, this workshop will be a disaster.

We arrive at the park. And it turns out that I needn't have worried.

Tallulah Gorge brushes the drizzle aside as a trifle of no consequence. Immediately and completely, Talullah pulls us into a wild and dazzling landscape; the effect is that of an electric jolt. From the first overlook on the North Rim Trail, the canyon captures us, drawing us to its brink to marvel at the sheer walls of granite and the bright fall trees on their heights and to peer into the white waters of the Tallulah River foaming far below.

One overlook after another lures us to the edge to lean over the guardrails and look down. At Inspiration Point the gorge drops almost one thousand feet. Farther up the trail, the falls of L'Eau d'Or tumble in three wild tiers, and, just beyond, Tempest Falls beckons like a mirage, framed by the vivid reds of sourwood and the bright yellow of wild grape. A long zigzag of metal stairs takes us down three hundred steps to a suspension bridge swaying over Hurricane Falls. We cross white-knuckled, grasping the railing as we swing just eighty feet above the roar of the falls below.

Breathing hard, we climb back up to the trail. Continuing our Tallulah tour at a restorative pace, we meet the smaller treasures of the park. They compete for our attention with the panoramic views from the trail—the blue globes of catbrier berries, rhododendrons pink in their second blooming, Maryland golden-aster, and the dainty blue asters as well, all wearing their fall raiment.

We come to a clearing and settle into the quiet while sitting on a few logs. Notebooks and pens in hand, we begin to write. I ask each of my pupils—we

OPPOSITE: *The rim of the gorge is lit with a red blaze of sourwood and the glow of gold leaves behind it. I removed every extraneous detail from the distant landscape, so the viewer's eye may follow the long bare twigs across the canyon to L'Eau d'Or Falls, its blue tiers glimmering in the shadows.*

are all students of nature—to select a small object that interests them. It can be anything—a twig, a flower, a leaf. Then I introduce them to the three prompts of nature journaling—"I notice," "I wonder," and "it reminds me of _____."

I find a striking fungus on a piece of dead wood. The edges of the fungus are hard, scalloped like a decorative bracket, and striped with mahogany. I start my journal page to demonstrate, sketching and writing with no particular method, in no particular order. I narrate what I am thinking as I work, showing the group right or wrong does not apply to the process. The seeing, the experience itself, is the goal.

I notice that my fungus grows in a bracket shape. I draw the edges, hard and scalloped. The plop of a raindrop falls on my shoulder as I work, a tiny cool missile, isolated in time.

Each student has bent over her selection to examine it.

I wonder whether the stripes on the fungus are like the rings of a tree, marking seasons of drought or water. I darken the chestnut stripes in my sketch. I'm pleased with my question and note it on the page. Behind me sounds the call of the blue jay, its insistent "Jay, jay!" ringing from the oaks.

It reminds me of a porch overhang! The tops of the fungus growths are darker than their bottoms and damp with rain. Perhaps they are a refuge for insects on a rainy day. I make the notes beside my drawing.

When we finish, we pass around our notebooks, appreciating each discovery in turn. Who knew a small twig could have its own resident spider, so tiny it lives in a crack in the bark? Or that a beetle's shell could have the iridescence of a rainbow?

Rejuvenated, we pack up our notebooks and continue to the South Rim Trail, crossing the river on the highway bridge built near the dam. The rocks below the dam are swirled in the telltale patterns of metamorphosis,

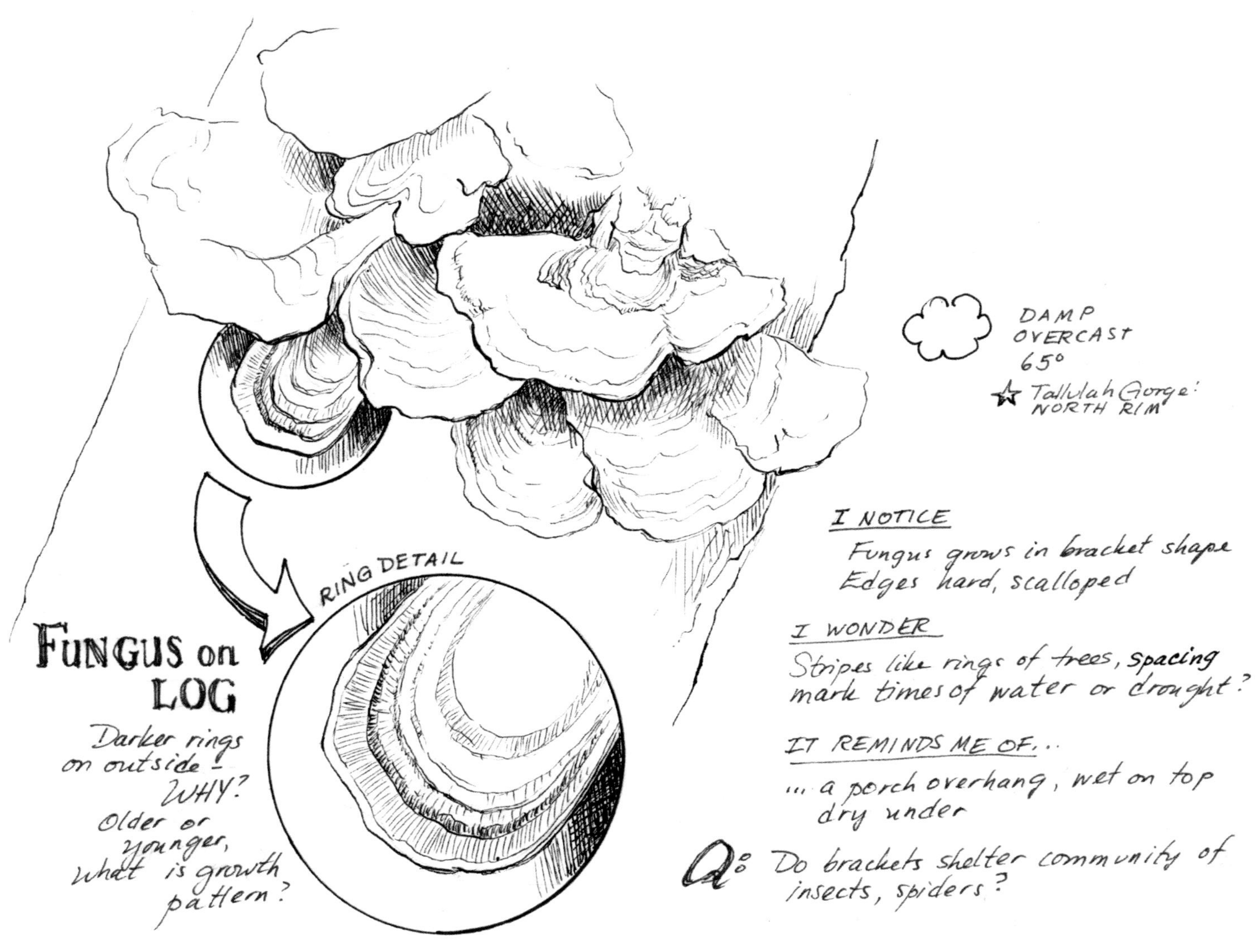
DAMP
OVERCAST
65°
Tallulah Gorge:
NORTH RIM
RING DETAIL
FUNGUS on
LOG
Darker rings
on outside -
WHY?
Older or
younger,
what is growth
pattern?
I NOTICE
Fungus grows in bracket shape
Edges hard, scalloped
I WONDER
Stripes like rings of trees, spacing
mark times of water or drought?
IT REMINDS ME OF...
... a porch overhang, wet on top
dry under
Q: Do brackets shelter community of
insects, spiders?

showing the sedimentary layers folded and re-formed by heat and pressure inside the earth.

We stop at a pavilion on the trail and again pull out our journals. We have a view across the gorge to the north rim and the trail we just traveled. I demonstrate a different journal tool by drawing a combination of map and overhead view. I sketch the sweep of the canyon bend as a bird might see it from above, adding the crazy tilted rocks of the canyon walls and the pointed triangles of pines clinging to the walls of the gorge. Next to it, I pen my question, "What earth force tilted these rocks, and how many ages did it take?" Beside us, a squirrel scampers through the pines at the cliff's edge. One slip is a fall of hundreds of feet. But he jumps fearlessly from branch to branch. Across the way, the south-facing cliff is green with pines. I note that on our side, the trees on the cliffs face the cooler north. I write, "Do different species grow in the shadows?"

The sky is still gray overhead. No matter.

We leave with a memory of Tallulah Gorge etched with sound and sight, smell and touch. Devoting attention to the natural world, we have been paid back tenfold with a rich experience of life.

—A. L.

July 18, 1970, was hot and sunny, and an anxious crowd of more than thirty thousand people, including Georgia's governor, stood at the rim of Tallulah Gorge to watch one of the most daring stunts ever performed by a human. The famed tightrope aerialist and acrobat Karl Wallenda was about to walk a thousand feet straight across the yawning chasm—on a ⅝-inch-thick steel cable strung nearly eight hundred feet above the canyon floor. The highwire was anchored to towers built for the event on each side of the gorge. The crowd held its collective breath as Wallenda mounted the cable and then tiptoed, stumbled, and even performed two handstands during his eighteen-minute walk across the chasm. Millions more people watched the stunt on television.

The daredevil feat brought instant worldwide fame to Tallulah Gorge.

Today thousands of people continue to visit the gorge, now the centerpiece of Tallulah Gorge State Park, which straddles Rabun and Habersham Counties in Northeast Georgia. They come now to hike the park's scenic trails and to get breathtaking, top-to-bottom views of the stunning gorge and its roaring waterfalls. Travel magazines from time to time describe the gorge as one of the state's most strikingly beautiful natural areas. Georgia lists it as one of the state's official Seven Natural Wonders.

The gorge is about two miles long and nearly one thousand feet deep at its deepest point. It is also narrow, only about a thousand feet across. Its sheer granite walls fall almost at a 90-degree angle from the land above. They form dramatic cliffs that amaze first-time visitors—and even those who have seen them many times.

Getting to the gorge's jagged boulder-strewn bottom requires negotiating a swaying suspension bridge and a steep staircase of 530 steps straight down the side of the canyon. A close-up view of one of Georgia's most spectacular waterfalls, Hurricane Falls, is the reward for those who make it to the bottom. Also at the bottom, the view of the canyon towering above is one of the Southeast's most impressive sights. Within and around the gorge is a plethora of wildflowers, birds, and animals. Three of Georgia's protected species—persistent trillium, monkey-face orchid, and the green salamander—live there.

The gorge's majestic cliffs are made of quartzite granite, one of Earth's hardest rocks. The rocks were at one time layers of sand covered by ocean waters. Over eons, the huge sand layers were compacted and cemented into sandstone rock. Then, under the tremendous heat and pressures of mountain building, the sandstone was transformed into quartzite. The Tallulah River, flowing eventually to the Savannah River, took millions of years to carve most of the gorge from the quartzite.

Tallulah Gorge, in fact, is a textbook example of an important geological phenomenon that helped shape most of the dramatic mountain scenery—magnificent waterfalls, rushing whitewater streams, deep gorges—of North Georgia. The phenomenon is known as stream capture. That process, mainly erosion over thousands to millions of years, diverts a stream or river from its own bed to flow instead down the bed of a neighboring stream. In essence, eroding streams are battling one another for supremacy, according to geologists. One such never-ending battle is between the Chattahoochee and the Tugaloo Rivers for dominance in North Georgia.

Tallulah Gorge formed over the past two million years (a short time in geologic terms) when the Tugaloo, a tributary of the Savannah River that flows to the Atlantic Ocean, eroded a ridge and "captured" the Tallulah River—which formerly flowed to the Chattahoochee and eventually the Gulf of Mexico. As it changed course, the swift-flowing Tallulah carved the gorge—a process still ongoing today.

When European settlers first laid eyes on the gorge in the early nineteenth century, the river hurtling through the chasm and the stupendous falls it created were even more awesome sights than they are today. The roar of the falls, it was said, could be heard miles away. Travel writers dubbed the falls the Niagara of the South. In the 1880s, a thriving tourist resort sprang up along the gorge, and a railroad was built to ferry in tourists from Atlanta and elsewhere to see the amazing falls. But then, around 1913, the predecessor of the Georgia Power Company permanently reduced the river's flow by building a 126-foot-high concrete dam upstream of the gorge. Activists had tried to stop the project from being built, but their efforts were for naught. After completion, the dam and its powerhouse supplied electricity for Atlanta's streetcars and industries. (The scenic sixty-three-acre lake created by the dam is now part of the state park.) By the 1920s, the resort built to accommodate tourists had withered away.

After that, the gorge received less attention, even though its astounding beauty had never faded. Wallenda's death-defying walk in 1970 showed that Tallulah Gorge was as awe-inspiring as ever, and the nature-loving crowds returned.

—C. S.

23 Amicalola Falls

Seven cascades form the third-highest waterfall east of the Mississippi

Six hundred steps to the top of Amicalola Falls in North Georgia's Dawson County.

Puffing, I paused halfway up the stairs scaling the third-highest falls in the eastern United States. My sister Jane, close behind, didn't seem to object. A symphony of birdsong and rushing water accompanied our climb, but it was difficult to enjoy. I was struggling to catch my breath.

After a minute's rest, my heart ceased its alarming pounding. We resumed our plodding ascent, carefully making only positive comments when our quad muscles burned. "This is a great workout" was the repeated descant.

Every few flights, we stopped to watch the great cascade of water tumbling down the mountainside. Tall trees clung to the slopes, framing the falls with freshly minted green, each view a reward for our climb.

Finally we reached the top, and any pain we felt became an insignificant nothing.

We stood on top of the world. Rolling to the edge of the horizon were waves of foothills lit with the sun's morning rays. At our feet, beneath the walkway bridge, the mighty torrent of the Amicalola roared down the mountainside into the shadows. We seemed perched on the very brink of the Blue Ridge and the eight-hundred-foot plunge to the Piedmont. Here, poised between water and sky, we felt as if we could leap down the mountain with the falls or fly into the air with the birds.

The view was intoxicating. We dawdled, leaning on the railing to watch as the sun slowly chased the dawn shadows across the hills. Surely, no other place could be like this, where one could stand on a waterfall and look down like a giant or a god surveying their realm below.

For the hike down, we skipped the stairs. A lovely alternate trail rambled through the woods beside the falls. The way was lit with the fiery glow of flame azalea blooming in the wild. This native shrub makes its appearance only in the acidic soils of the southern Appalachians, and here it raised its regal candelabras of red and orange as though to light our descent from the sky.

OPPOSITE: *The strong divide between shadow and light in this scene created a compositional challenge: how to carry the eye across that boundary to move freely through the painting. Stairsteps of foaming water invite the viewer down the rush of Amicalola Falls and into the shadows, from which the eye can trace the billows of trees up into the sunlit Piedmont, then back into the painting through the branches at the top.*

Vivid greens and fiery reds make this painting of flame azalea a study in complementary colors. The two shades vibrate against one another, creating an intensity in place of strong contrast between light and dark. On the left, I cooled the greens with blue, a method that pushes elements into the background, creating distance.

The Little Amicalola Creek flowed onward from the base of the falls. We clambered around the rocks and dabbled in the water, turning over pretty stones and peering up at the falls a final time, their full height of more than seven hundred feet shrouded from view by trees and the ziggurat of its seven cascades. Now breathing easily, we listened to Amicalola's music of birdsong and water.

We returned home to savor a cup full of beauty, flavored, admittedly, with a small taste of satisfaction—

Feeling virtuous about the workout.

—A. L.

Thousands of visitors come to Amicalola Falls State Park each year to see its spectacular waterfall. Plunging 729 feet over seven cascades from top to bottom, it's the highest waterfall in Georgia—four times higher than Niagara Falls. The remarkable features make it one of Georgia's official Seven Natural Wonders.

Hardy long-distance hikers know Amicalola Falls State Park for another reason: it's the jumping-off point for the famed Appalachian Trail, the marvelous hiking path that extends 2,190 miles from Georgia to Maine. An 8.5-mile approach trail begins in the park and leads to Springer Mountain, the Appalachian Trail's southern terminus. In the park, an iconic, oft-photographed stone archway marks the beginning of the approach trail.

In its long rugged course to its northern terminus at Mount Katahdin, Maine, the Appalachian Trail traverses the wild scenic, wooded, pastoral, and culturally resonant lands of its eponymous mountain range, which also encompasses the outstanding Blue Ridge Mountains.

But to gain an appreciation of such natural magnificence, one need go no farther than the overlook—or "plunge point"—at the very top of Amicalola Falls, where the waterfall begins its long descent to the bottom. From the top, the astonishing views of mountains, valleys, and plunging falls below can leave one breathless. The overlook affords a view of the southern edge of the rugged Blue Ridge Mountains as they step down into the rolling Piedmont. Those who feel up to it can start at the bottom of the falls and take a trail to the 604-step staircase that takes visitors to the summit. A pause midway at a viewing platform gives visitors an enchanting look at the roaring water. Another option is to drive up to the parking lot at the top and from there take a short walk to the overlook—and then perhaps descend the staircase to the viewing platform.

Forming the breathtaking falls is Amicalola Creek, a tributary of the Etowah River. The creek plunges over and down the steep slope—or escarpment—that marks the edge of the Blue Ridge Mountains. Over eons the creek eroded the escarpment and carved out the series of seven dramatic cascades. The waterfall today plunges from an elevation of more than twenty-four hundred feet to the foot of the escarpment at seventeen hundred feet.

At the bottom, the creek flows into a picturesque, trout-filled reflecting pool, where anglers try their luck. The water, cooled by its lengthy tumble down the slope, is suitable for trout, which favor clean chilled water.

Before the nineteenth century, European settlers knew little about the wondrous waterfall. It lay within the expansive wild territory of the Cherokee people, who in ancient times had migrated from the Great Lakes to the Southeast.

William Williamson, a Georgia surveyor who explored the Cherokee lands in 1832, produced one of the first written accounts of the falls. He wrote:

> In the course of my route in the Mountains I discovered a Water Fall perhaps the greatest in the World. the most majestic Scene that I have ever witnessed or heard of. the Creek passes over the mountain & the fall [which] I think can't be less than Six hundred Yards. The Mountain is at least three-fourths of a mile high. I made great exertions to get on the summit, but the ascent was so great that I was completely exhausted by the time I reached half way. My position was such that I had a perfect view of the entire Fall. The Stream is Called *Um-ma-eolola* from the Fall (Tumbling Waters).

Williamson may have exaggerated some of the heights, but his awe of the falls' great beauty was genuine.

Eventually, the Cherokee would lose their homeland. In 1835, a group of men claiming to be leaders of the Cherokee Nation signed the Treaty of New Echota with the United States. In 1838, under terms of the treaty, the U.S. government forced thousands of Cherokee to move to Indian Territory west of the Mississippi River. Their mass removal came to be known as the Trail of Tears because of the brutal hardships they faced along the way. Many died during the harrowing journey. In an oft-told story, one Cherokee woman refused to leave and hid out at Amicalola Falls until the 1850s.

The wholesale removal of the Cherokee opened the Georgia mountains to settlement by white people, but the terrain around Amicalola Falls proved too rugged for farming. In 1852 an entrepreneur named Bartley Crane built a water-powered mill on Little Amicalola Creek near the base of the falls. Eight years later, Methodists established a campground nearby as a place where people could gather for all-day picnics and preaching.

Remarkably, the gristmill survived the Civil War and continued to operate into the early twentieth century. Georgia purchased the falls in 1911 and in 1940 bought the land surrounding the falls from the Crane family. The state designated the property Amicalola Falls State Park, the state's twelfth state park. The park, however, would remain mostly undeveloped until 1958, when the Georgia Appalachian Trail Club decided to move the southern terminus of the trail from Mount Oglethorpe to nearby Springer Mountain. The club then blazed the approach trail from Amicalola Falls to the top of Springer Mountain, so that Appalachian Trail hikers would be able to access the trail from a major highway.

Today Amicalola Falls is one of Georgia's most popular state parks, drawing visitors from all over the state and Southeast as well. The jaw-dropping waterfall is still the main attraction, but miles of well-maintained trails take visitors through stately forests and other natural mountain habitats. Visitors can camp in the park, staying in one of several cabins or stay in a grand comfortable lodge operated by a private management company through an agreement with the state. From the top of the falls, a five-mile trail also leads to the Len Foote Hike Inn, a popular eco-friendly lodge at an elevation of more than three thousand feet; the inn is only accessible to visitors on foot.

Whether one goes for a short hike or a stay of several days, Amicalola Falls State Park is a must-see phenomenon that should be on everyone's bucket list for seeing natural Georgia.

—C. S.

24 Richard Russell Scenic Highway

A winding way through mountain heights

We are headed home. Five women with backpacks and overnight bags are sandwiched in the rear of my van as we leave Tallulah Gorge. Friends and students, they have come for my weekend workshop, The Art of the Nature Journal.

Over the past three days, we've hiked miles of trail, examined everything from bugs to canyon walls, observed, drawn, and journaled. Now we are ready to play. Our reward is a leisurely Sunday drive along the famous Richard Russell Scenic Highway through North Georgia's Blue Ridge Mountains. Happily, our path will cross the Chattahoochee National Forest with views of the peaks of the Blue Ridge Divide. We have arrived just as the high season for fall color kicks off.

We left behind the bustle of life while we were away and attuned ourselves to the slower pace of nature. What will we enjoy of this mountain country as we rush past at seventy miles per hour?

An hour passes as we cross North Georgia, bypassing the state's highest peak, Brasstown Bald, for the promise of the byway's vistas. The sun bursts into a clear blue sky as we begin our drive on the Richard Russell Scenic Highway.

The road earns its name. A marvel of modern civil engineering, it skates through mountains that were notched with explosives and carved by great

OPPOSITE: *Fall trees form a parade of passing color along the Richard Russell Scenic Highway. Here, the bright foliage spills down through the shadows, guiding the eye into the gloom to spot the lights of the car ahead, glimmering in the twilight. The golden tree emerges here as it appeared to me, like a torch lighting the road before us.*

earth-moving machines. The road path swoops and banks, propelling us from peak to peak and through the vales between—as a bird might fly if it took wing in these mountains. Fall colors flicker and fly past, first one side, then the other, lighting up the slopes. I'm grateful to my friend Yasmin for volunteering to drive—my head swivels with the others in the car as we take turns pointing, oohing and ahhing at each beautiful view or bright tree.

We pull over at the first promising overlook and get out. We are on a grassy shelf beside the highway.

Young tulip poplars frame the view in shadowy verticals. Away and beyond is the sunlit tapestry of the mountains, green folds threaded with golds and reds—poplars, sourwoods, and maples. Later in the fall, oaks and hickories will add their burnished shades.

Beneath this cloak of trees, the mountains recede in endless layers, each increasingly blue-tinted with the slow exhalation of trees. The haze of blue is from natural hydrocarbons released by the forest. The Blue Ridge is the southernmost range in the Appalachian Mountains, one of the oldest ranges in the world, raised hundreds of millions of years ago in a collision of Earth's great continental plates, North America and Africa. The impact of the clashing plates thrust the mountains into the sky, as hard rock folded like bread dough.

All this geologic drama is hidden beneath the lovely cover of trees the land now wears in its sedate old age.

We dawdle at the overlook, drinking in the color and air and sunlight.

We resume our drive, finding ourselves traveling through alternating shadows and sunlight. Gold pillars of poplar catch the sun like torches on the mountain. At the next overlook, a red oak, once majestic, stands broken, with branches lying on the ground around it. These mountains, so beautiful this clear fall day, also bring storms and ice, lightning, and pitiless winds.

Dukes Creek Falls is our final stop, where we savor the last of the afternoon. A trail of stairs and overlooks passes through a leafy filigree of orange and gold, the falls at the end a sheet of glittering white against the lacy black of overhanging hemlocks.

The weekend is over. We head for home.

When the naturalist William Bartram came to North Georgia more than two centuries ago, he traveled on horseback, by canoe, and when necessary on foot, exploring what was then the land of the Cherokee Nation. He journeyed through an unmapped wilderness.

Our path along the Richard Russell Scenic Highway was not rustic. Yet we were privileged to stand on mountains and see faraway peaks, shadowed dales and sunlit waterfalls, to behold in an afternoon a landscape that no person in times past could have seen in a lifetime.

—A. L.

The Richard Russell Scenic Highway, running across the superb Blue Ridge Mountains in North Georgia's White and Union Counties, has been called a passage to splendor. Dipping, rising, winding, and curving through the lush Chattahoochee National Forest, it takes travelers across some of Georgia's most awesome mountain scenery. Along the way, it provides access to majestic waterfalls, clear-running streams, sweeping mountain vistas, and rugged hiking paths, including the famed Appalachian Trail.

The highway was, in fact, designed and built in large part during the 1960s for the purpose of leisure travel and recreation to help weary souls escape—at least temporarily—the hustle and bustle of everyday life. Since then the twisting, turning roadway has become one of Georgia's most remarkably beautiful routes—some say *the* most beautiful.

The highway (Georgia 348) originally was named for the late Richard B. Russell, who represented Georgia in the U.S. Senate from 1933 until 1971, when he died in office. At the time of his death, he was one of the most powerful legislators in the U.S. Congress, serving at various times as Senate president pro tem and chairing several important committees. He was a close friend and strong supporter of President Franklin D. Roosevelt, whose administration implemented scores of public works projects—such as the Blue Ridge Parkway—that enabled millions of Americans to access and enjoy natural areas. In a similar vein, Russell was a solid proponent of building the scenic highway through the mountains of his home state.

But before the route was named for Russell, it was a rugged, treacherous wagon trail that early settlers used for traveling over Hogpen Gap, the highest point along the trail that ran between the settlements of Choestoe and Helen. Today's paved highway roughly follows the old wagon route. It begins at the intersection with Georgia Alternate 75 near beautiful Smithgall Woods State Park and then ascends steeply to the west. It forms the northern boundary of the eastern half of the Raven Cliffs Wilderness, offering access to two picturesque waterfalls, Raven Cliff Falls (chapter 34) and Duke's Creek Falls. Two places along the highway provide access to the Appalachian Trail.

Mountain overlooks along the road provide splendid views of the Raven Cliffs Wilderness Area and the Tray Mountain Wilderness Area. One overlook looks down on the Dahlonega gold belt, where the precious metal was first discovered in 1828 and triggered Georgia's gold rush a year later. In the distance rises majestic Mount Yonah with its huge dramatic cliff face.

A short distance up the road is the highway's highest point, Hogpen Gap, elevation 3,485 feet—with a view of one of Georgia's most magnificent mountain vistas. Hogpen Gap has another distinction: it marks the Blue Ridge Divide. Water flowing west from here drains into the Tennessee River, and water flowing east runs into the Chattahoochee River. In addition, Hogpen Gap is one of two places where the Appalachian Trail crosses the highway.

The overlook at Hogpen Gap provides a view of a majestic valley called Lordamercy Cove, supposedly named for its difficult terrain. Some locals also say the name comes from the exclamation people utter when they first see the unspoiled vista. Still another story holds that the name originated with settlers in mule-drawn wagons traveling the original old dirt trail. For them, Hogpen Gap was especially treacherous. Wagon brakes were notoriously poor, not reliable when making the steep descent from the gap. To remedy the problem, wagon drivers would stop to cut down timber before descending. Then they would tie a log or two behind the wagon to slow it on the downhill journey. Sometimes the logs would get hung up by a rock or another obstacle and cause all kinds of problems. The predicament, some locals say, would elicit cries of "Lord 'a' mercy."

Hogpen Gap has one other noteworthy natural feature. Directly across the road from the overlook is a stunning sheer cliff—nearly sixty feet high in some places—of banded gneiss, a metamorphic rock that's the most common rock in the eastern Blue Ridge. The amazing rock wall stretches several hundred feet along the highway. During most of the year, water dripping from springs keeps the natural wall moist, creating a unique habitat in which certain ferns and wildflowers thrive. The cliff saxifrage is a wildflower that roots in cracks in the rock. It produces small, delicate white flowers adorned with red and yellow dots that seem like dancers when buffeted by a breeze.

In the dead of winter, the dripping water often freezes, forming a dramatically long wall of solid ice along the highway. The ice wall is an attraction in itself for photographers and casual visitors, but it is especially alluring to a particular group of outdoor enthusiasts, ice climbers. They come to the frozen wall to hone their ice-climbing skills and enjoy their pastime.

In 2000, the Richard Russell Scenic Highway became part of an even longer scenic route in Georgia's mountains, the Russell-Brasstown National Scenic Byway. The forty-mile loop route now connects the Richard Russell Scenic Highway to other nearby roads that also wind through the Chattahoochee forest—and offers access to other splendid waterfalls, trails, and breathtaking vistas, including Georgia's highest peak, Brasstown Bald (see chapter 26).

—C. S.

25 Cloudland Canyon

Thousand-foot-deep canyons, sandstone cliffs, and cascading waterfalls

It was spring when I planned my visit to Cloudland Canyon, a place Charlie Seabrook described as one of "Georgia's most scenic parks." I hoped the seasonal rains would work their magic in bringing the park's many waterfalls to life.

This was early in my travels to the sites on Charlie's list. I invited my neighbor Yasmin, who had expressed interest in coming on my next nature outing. She had surprised me. Yasmin was a city person. As the child of immigrants, an Iraqi father and Austrian mother, she had grown up working the family gas station in Chicago. In our neighborhood circle in Georgia, Yasmin was known for savvy shopping and serving dinners of delectable Arabic dishes, recipes passed down from her father.

But a companion for a nature trip? I wondered. Earlier in the year, her father had died, and Yasmin seemed to still be deep in grief. I hoped the outing would lift her spirits.

We reached the boundary of the park in Georgia's extreme northwest corner in early morning; the road became markedly steeper as we approached the entrance. Perhaps—as the park's name suggested—we were ascending to some lofty realm high above the earth.

The popular Overlook Trail beckoned. It promised grand views and an easy half-mile walk. Yasmin had brought her young golden retriever, and the trail seemed a good choice for a puppy on a leash.

A short stroll brought us to the main overlook. Surely the view should not have been a surprise, yet I was unprepared for the vast canvas of sky and earth unfurling at the brink of the chasm. The canyon yawned wide, winding in broad curves to a far horizon. The vista, all sky and earth, seemed more like the landscapes of the West than our gentle southern mountains. Nonetheless, it was the South, too—lines of lush trees had found a foothold on ledges on the steep walls, thereby softening the rocky layers of the canyon.

Our eyes flicked from trail to canyon as we made our way along the trail, the huge arc of the sky irresistibly drawing our gaze again and again. Far below was Sitton Gulch Creek, carving its ancient way through the shadows of the canyon. Above, the clifftops were rimmed with sunlight.

Across the canyon, a waterfall, rushing and roaring with spring rains, cascaded hundreds of feet down a steep cliff wall. Along the trail, dogwood raised its white branches to make a kind of lace across the view. Wild azalea, waist high, invited us to smell its scent and finger pink satin petals. Blossoms of wild blueberries, rose and white, hung like small bells from diminutive bushes on the forest floor.

At the final overlook at trail's end, an astounding thousand-foot drop opened at our feet. The morning sun illuminated its layers like the pages of a book, telling Earth's long tale: golden sandstone from an age when this place was shallow sea and dark crumbling shale marking long-forgotten shoreline.

Yasmin was quiet, lingering at the fence for long minutes. "I didn't know this was here. I had no idea it was so beautiful." She paused, and I saw her eyes were wet. "I should have brought my father here."

OPPOSITE: *Layers of glowing sandstone mark the history of Cloudland Canyon, from eons when the land lay beneath a shallow sea. The painting reflects my impression of the intense interplay of cool blue shadow and warm golden light across the canyon.*

The view from an overlook is of a distant waterfall roaring down the cliff across the way. Framed by the lacy curtains of dogwood, the falls appeared as a miniature cinema picture flickering across the far cliff wall. For this painting, I sprinkled salt into the green washes between the dogwoods; the salt crystals pushed the pigment aside to suggest blossom shapes layered through the branches.

As we drove home, Yasmin professed her desire to see more, and at that moment we made a pact to take the next trip together. It was the beginning of many Georgia natural wonder trips to come.

Nature steals into the soul with no warning. Sometimes all it takes is one meeting, and it opens someone's heart to beauty, to healing.

And, if one is so fortunate, to unexpected friendship.

—A. L.

Hemlock Falls cascades into a pool that is tinged turquoise by the minerals in the water. Here I allowed grains of dark watercolor to create the rough texture of the rock, with a translucent wash of green to evoke the glow of the water. A few lines suggest the trees and leaves in the foreground, allowing the viewer to enter the scene and complete it in the mind's eye.

From the overlook spot called the Point along the east rim of Cloudland Canyon, one can see the wide rugged gorge as it gives way in the distance to Lookout Valley with its peaceful pastures and fertile forests. The view is one of Georgia's most gorgeous natural vistas. The panoramic scene alone is worth a visit to Cloudland Canyon State Park.

But equally worth a trip is a descent into the steep-walled chasm itself. The Waterfalls Trail, with six hundred metal steps and boardwalks bordering a sheer cliff, takes visitors down to the canyon's boulder-strewn floor nearly a thousand feet below. On the way down, the trail provides access to two short spur trails, both of which run through a moist forest and end at a mighty waterfall—Cherokee Falls midway down and Hemlock Falls near the bottom.

Fed by Daniel Creek, the falling torrents of water are two of Georgia's most photogenic waterfalls as they cascade across layers of sandstone and shale and end in picturesque pools below. Cherokee Falls drops dramatically about sixty feet over an expansive, eye-catching rock wall into its pool. Farther down, Hemlock Falls plunges about ninety feet into another pool on the canyon floor.

The park also boasts open fields, hardwood forests, roaring creeks, and wild caves; at 3,485 acres, it is one of Georgia's largest parks.

Accounting for all the superb beauty is Cloudland Canyon's amazing geology, which makes it one of Georgia's most stunning natural areas. The canyon, in fact, is an excellent place to learn the geology that formed the jaw-dropping vistas and rugged terrain of Georgia's northwest corner. The trail down to the canyon floor takes the visitor through millions of years of geologic time: each step is onto progressively older rocks.

Cloudland Canyon's name, however, comes from the low-hanging clouds that occasionally caress its rims and dip into its gaping expanse. The gorge is located on the western edge of Lookout Mountain, a distinct prominence in the Appalachian Plateau (or Cumberland Plateau) that rises about one thousand feet above surrounding areas in the region.

Lookout Mountain itself was created through a combination of tectonic activity and erosion—uplifted during the period of mountain building that formed the Appalachians, known as the Appalachian orogeny. More than three hundred million years ago, all of Lookout Mountain lay beneath a primordial ocean. When the ocean receded, rushing, scouring streams atop the mountain began eroding the sandstone and limestone rock that make up most of the mountain.

Those streams today are Daniel Creek and Bear Creek, which converge to form Sitton Gulch Creek, which runs the entire length of the canyon. Through relentless erosion over eons, Sitton Gulch Creek and its tributaries formed the gorge that now is the signature feature of Cloudland Canyon State Park. Geologists say that the canyon is a dramatic example of the power of a stream to cut downward through rocks broken by natural fractures. As such, Cloudland Canyon has nearly perpendicular sandstone cliffs and slopes that drop more than one thousand feet to the valley below.

All this provides for a wide variety of ecosystems—high cliffs and bluffs of sandstone above and creeks, ravines, and wild caves with exposed limestone on the slopes and canyon below. Cloudland, in fact, is Georgia's only state park with caves. The visitor also will find dense, rich forests—some of them old growth—in the coves and on north-facing slopes. Shortleaf and Virginia pines cling precariously to footholds on the cliffs' ledges. The variety of ecosystems makes the park a floral haven, home to thousands of species of native trees, shrubs, wildflowers, vines, ferns, and mosses.

In 1938 the State of Georgia purchased about nineteen hundred acres from private landowners of what was then known as Sitton's Gulch. A year later it was designated Cloudland Canyon State Park. A Civilian Conservation Corps project during the Great Depression built the first facilities, access roads, and signs for the new park. Its expansion has continued to its present size of more than thirty-four hundred acres.

Until 1939 the only access to the area (and much of Dade County) was through Tennessee or Alabama. That year Georgia began work on Highway 136 to connect U.S. 41 to the new park. The difficulty of accessing much of the terrain meant that most of the mountainous land that became the park had avoided the ravages of industrialization, logging, and development that beset many other natural areas.

The isolation also safeguarded the park's superb floral diversity. The park's seven trails provide views of most of this natural variety. Along the most popular route, the staircased Waterfalls Trail, plants adorn just about every nook and crevice in the boulders and sheer rock cliff bordering the trail. Other environments along the way range from wet to dry. A large, dry rock outcrop at the trail's start supports mountain spleenwort, partridgeberry, hairy bush-honeysuckle, mountain laurel, Catawba rhododendron, red maple, and trailing arbutus. As the steep trail descends, colonies of sedges, ferns, blooming foamflower, and saxifrage thrive in hanging gardens thanks to a constant stream of water from the upper ridges of the canyon. The water moves downward through porous stone, seeps out, and moistens the rock wall.

A hike along the 2.5-mile Sitton Gulch Trail running parallel to the creek on the canyon floor in early spring introduces visitors to the lush bright blooms of dozens of native wildflower species. Encouraging the abundant growth is the fossil-bearing limestone on the canyon bottom. Two of Cloudland's wild limestone caves—Sittons and Case—are open to occasional tours led by expert cavers.

So, fair warning: from mind-boggling vistas to dazzling waterfalls to a kaleidoscope of wildflower color, Cloudland Canyon State Park may leave a visitor spellbound.

—C. S.

26 Brasstown Bald

Georgia's highest mountain offers a view of four states

Rain clouds followed me north.

It was early November, still the season of high color in northeastern Georgia's Blue Ridge Mountains. I'd been checking the weather all week, looking for a clear forecast at sunrise. My plan was to stay in the mountains overnight and catch the sun's first light on the fall foliage from Georgia's highest peak—Brasstown Bald.

The afternoon clouds cleared as I approached the mountain, releasing the sun to trace the treetops with light. I decided to take an impromptu detour to the mountaintop—perhaps I would catch a glorious sunset too.

The car hugged the curves of the road to the top. But with each turn, the light grew dimmer; a cloud had descended on the mountain. Near the peak, wind and a freezing rain began to beat on the windshield, and I found myself in a raging fall storm.

I turned back. A clear sunrise now seemed unlikely.

I was staying at a mountain home dubbed Meditation House. The larger guest rooms, named Love and Joy, were already booked, so I had reserved a room on the lower floor, Tranquility, that shared a bathroom with Peace. Luckily, Peace was unoccupied, so I had the bathroom to myself.

OPPOSITE: *The foliage of oaks and other hardwoods forms a rich carpet of color on Brasstown Bald, re-created here with washes of watercolor pigment allowed to merge freely on the paper. A layer of ink lines defines the forms of the trees themselves, with blue drips of watercolor evoking the lacy network of shadows cast by the morning sun.*

I went to bed reflecting that the day had brought neither tranquility nor peace, let alone love and joy. I hoped for better in the morning.

When the alarm roused me for the drive to the peak, it was still dark. Thick mists shrouded the road, and the path through the dense wall of fog was slow.

Finally, near the top, the day began to lighten, and as I rounded a bend, I suddenly drove out of the low-lying clouds into glorious light: sunrise on Brasstown Bald.

I pounded the steps to the observation deck two at a time. I didn't want to miss a moment of this glorious light.

I had arrived in heaven. The sky above was clear like the dawn of the world, the new sun lighting a strange land below, nearly submerged in a sea of clouds. White waves rolled to the edge of the horizon in every direction, rose tinted and blue shadowed in their valleys.

The peaks of the surrounding mountains rose in islands, red oaks aflame in the sun's first light.

I circled the observation deck. Every time I stopped, I seemed to encounter a world I had never seen before.

As the hour passed, the sun burned the clouds away, and I could see more of the mountain peaks. At my feet, the remnants of the night's snow lay in small drifts as it melted into morning dew.

I left the deck to circle the top of the mountain, to see the wild brambles below the peak iced with frost. Icicles clung in the shadows, weighing down leaves still bright with green.

When I returned to the deck for a final look, I found I was no longer alone. A young couple greeted me with beaming smiles. They asked if I would take their photo—they had just gotten engaged.

Brimming with joy, they smiled their love, and the peace and tranquility of the ancient mountains lit up behind them, young again in the morning of a new day.

The mountain had brought every promised gift.

—A. L.

The bright leaves of Heuchera villosa *drip with icicles after an early November storm. On its cool north side, Brasstown Bald harbors native plants found more commonly at more northern latitudes.*

OPPOSITE: *Oaks and evergreens light up the foreground of this painting, while a mountain peak in the background creates space and distance. This painting pays homage to the Asian landscape tradition, which often shows mountains and other natural features separated by mists to evoke the illusion of space on the flat plane of the paper.*

Brasstown Bald is neither brassy nor a town. Georgia's highest mountain lies within the Chattahoochee National Forest and straddles the border between Towns and Union Counties; its peak is in Towns County.

The name Brasstown probably derives from a misinterpretation of the Cherokee name Itse'yi, meaning "green place," that European settlers confused with the name Untsai'yi, meaning "brass."

Ecologically, Brasstown's summit is known as a bald, a characteristic of the highest mountain peaks in the southern Appalachians. Balds are covered primarily with dense growths of stunted vegetation and a few trees where one might expect a thick forest.

Depending on their vegetation, two types of mountain balds occur in the region—the grassy bald and the heath bald. Brasstown Bald is a heath bald—its summit is enveloped in native low-growing evergreens and shrubs such as mountain laurel and rhododendron. Heath balds typically occur where the soil is thin and well drained or is highly acidic, which stymies the growth of trees and other large woody plants. Mountain laurel and rhododendron are among the few shrubs that can survive on the cool thin soils atop Brasstown.

Like most other mountain balds in the southern Appalachians, Brasstown offers a breathtaking, unobstructed 360-degree view of the surrounding terrain. From the outside observation deck of the stone visitors center at the top, a clear day provides views of Georgia, North Carolina, South Carolina, and Tennessee. On good days in late September and October, it's even possible to see Atlanta's skyline about eighty-five miles away.

Totally clear days, however, are often hard to come by on Brasstown Bald. Because of its high elevation, the mountain experiences weather conditions different from the valleys and surrounding terrain below—Brasstown's is more like the weather of New England. The temperatures at the top may be cooler by ten to fifteen degrees or more, even on hot summer days. Strong wind and rain, as well as cooler temperatures, are not uncommon; fog, mist, and storms may move in unexpectedly and obscure the view.

Brasstown Bald's cool microclimate makes it the southernmost habitat for many northern plants and animals, such as the red-backed vole, a small, mouse-like creature that seldom inhabits elevations below three thousand feet. Just below Brasstown Bald's summit, an impressive northern hardwood forest of huge old yellow birches covers the north face of the mountain. The late Georgia naturalist Charles Wharton said he was incredulous when he first saw "the hoary beauty of the great birch forest on the north face of Brasstown Bald." Because of the mountain's atmospheric conditions, the trees and other vegetation of the forest are bathed for prolonged periods by mist, fog, and moisture-laden clouds—making it what's known as a cloud forest, the only one in Georgia. The continuous moisture from the clouds causes the old birches to be festooned with an attractive lichen known as old man's beard.

Heath balds such as Brasstown's also are associated with so-called boulderfields, which usually occur on north-facing slopes above thirty-two hundred feet. They consist of tightly packed boulders as large as ten feet in diameter—a result of severe freeze-thaw cycles that broke up big slabs of rock during glaciations about twenty thousand years ago. The cool temperatures associated with these sites help promote the growth of thick mosses, wildflowers, and northern ferns. The trees that manage to take root there are usually stunted and twisted.

Even so, the combination of moss-cloaked boulders and gnarled old trees creates a striking beauty like no other natural environment in Georgia. In *Natural Communities of Georgia*, Leslie Edwards, Jonathan Ambrose, and L. Katherine Kirkman write that the north-facing portion of Brasstown Bald "contains perhaps Georgia's best expression of northern hardwood and boulderfield forests."

The cloud-bathed forests, moss-covered boulderfields, outstanding spring and fall wildflower displays, and the spectacular views from the summit draw multitudes of visitors to Brasstown Bald each year. They come especially in the fall, when the summit as well as lower elevations provide magnificent views of fall leaf color.

Four hiking trails—all of which begin from Brasstown Bald's large paved parking lot—afford visitors the opportunity to scrutinize the mountain's natural treasures and splendors. Naturalists especially recommend the Wagon Train Trail, an old wagon road, that goes through the fantastic cloud forest near the summit, passing the rugged cliffs and boulderfields. In the boulderfields, rock tripe (an edible lichen that grows on rocks), other lichens, reindeer moss, old man's beard, and club moss thrive. Thick moss mats cover the boulders. Among the big rocks are yellow birches, basswoods, striped maples, witch hazel (small flowering trees), mountain maples, mountain hollies, and other trees. In early spring, silver bell, serviceberry, mountain buttercups, white saxifrage, toothwort, cinquefoil, bluets, violets, trilliums, and other wildflowers bloom along the trail.

The half-mile Summit Trail leads to the excellent visitors center at the top. Along the trail in spring and fall visitors are likely to encounter birds that prefer high altitudes—black and white warblers, black-throated green warblers, veeries, and winter wrens. The rhododendron thickets along the trail provide shelter for the rose-breasted grosbeak, which prefers to nest at elevations above three thousand feet.

It all makes Brasstown Bald not only Georgia's highest mountain but also one of the state's most magnificent wild places.

—C. S.

27 Rabun Bald

A mountain wilderness perched on the Eastern Continental Divide

"Do you hike alone?"

My fork is loaded with the last bite of my breakfast, homemade crepes with blueberry sauce. I put it down. The couple that runs the inn where I spent the night are curious about my Georgia natural wonders project. The husband wants details.

"Do you hike alone?"

"Sometimes, yes," I say. "I have to schedule trips around the weather—and not everybody's flexible on the last-minute stuff."

He nods.

I hadn't thought much about it until now. The more popular trails don't typically allow for a solitary hike. Other hikers are always around—safety in numbers, right? Anyway, I like hiking alone. I can sit for an hour and sketch a flower or mossy log. Or walk around taking photos of a scene from a dozen angles. Or even stand stock-still, squinting for long minutes until the landscape in front of me melts into blobs of light and color, and I can visualize the painting I want to make.

It's a gorgeous fall morning, the peak weekend for leaf-watching in northeast Georgia. I've been looking forward to this hike on Rabun Bald, the second-highest peak in Georgia, for weeks. And now, suddenly, I'm scared.

My imagination is spitting out doomsday scenarios of the hike I planned for this part of the Chattahoochee National Forest. Bears. Wild dogs. Rattlesnake bites, broken bones, gangs, crazy loners.

I load my suitcase into the car and fish a bright yellow canister out of the glove compartment. It's an ancient pepper spray, purchased for me by my husband early in our marriage, when I worked in downtown Atlanta. I carefully point the canister away from me and squeeze. A healthy stream shoots out. Within seconds, a few aerosolized droplets make their way into my lungs and I am coughing.

Yes! Thirty-year-old pepper spray. Still works. Check.

Armed and dangerous, I am ready to enjoy my solitary Sunday morning hike.

Rabun Bald is Brasstown Bald's lesser-known sibling. Unlike Brasstown Bald, Rabun remains largely untouched. No paved road or walkway leads to its peak. I will travel through a forest that remembers the past, a time before mountains were cleared for timber, vacation homes, or even visitor centers for well-meaning tourists.

The trailhead for Beegum Gap sits on a dead-end street lined with private homes. My guidebook reminds me not to block a driveway when I park.

I begin the climb. In just a few moments, I have stepped into a world of incandescent golds. The forest is flooded with light, a kaleidoscope of the sun shifting in a thousand facets through the foliage overhead. Even the forest floor is gold, fern fronds tracing golden curves on a carpet of fallen leaves. I am climbing a tower of light.

Soon the access trail reaches Bartram Trail, turning south toward the summit. I'm following in the steps of William Bartram, the writer and naturalist who traveled these mountains in the late 1700s. A shadowy glade of miniature trees, twisted trunks of rhododendron, raises a dark roof of leaves

OPPOSITE: *Rhododendron arches over the trail, making a window for the streaming morning sunlight on Rabun Bald. The placement of the central tree threatened to divide the painting in two—breaking a cardinal rule of composition—so I dissolved its strong vertical into the sun to allow the viewer's eye to move across the painting.*

over my path. Mossy rocks and glossy leaves of galax spread at their feet. I imagine he saw some of the same.

A raucous din sounds from the trail ahead—voices. The feeling of vulnerability returns. I reach into my pocket and grip the pepper spray. I am utterly alone. If someone seems menacing, will I say something first—or shoot?

As I round a bend in the trail, I see a troop of small boys—scouts, some in full uniform, tromping merrily toward me. A few say, "Hi" in shy, polite voices. Two dad types bring up the rear, smiling as we pass one another.

I feel foolish. Enough with the paranoia. Now the incline is steeper, and I concentrate on the climb—a series of grueling switchbacks and then the final ascent. The trail emerges on the peak and into a world of sky. A small observation deck sits on a stone foundation, the remains of a historic fire tower, I learn later.

The tower exerts an inexorable pull, and I climb the steep steps to the top for an astounding view—a 360-degree panorama of the horizon. I am perched on the great ridge of the Eastern Continental Divide. To the north are the mountains of North Carolina, where rivers run westward, entering the Tennessee River, the Mississippi, and ultimately the Gulf of Mexico. To the south are the peaks of Georgia and the Piedmont, where waters channel eastward into the Chattooga River, then the Savannah, and finally the Atlantic Ocean.

Somehow, Rabun Bald seems wilder and bigger than the taller Brasstown Bald.

A lone red oak struggles in the elements on the peak of Rabun Bald. I saw its broken form as a kind of ghost, clinging to life beneath a sweep of wild sky. Its bare shape makes a strong contrast to the riot of fall leaves, blueberry, and wild grasses that thrive at the top of the bald. The blue of surrounding mountains hovers at the horizon line.

I climb down from the observation platform to explore the peak. Stunted red oaks struggle in the thin soil, limbs and trunks thickened by lightning, wind, the ice of winter storms. I wander between rocks and golden grasses, wading, waist high, through a fiery mountaintop bouquet. Oak leaves are flame red and blueberry bushes crimson in the cool fall nights. The gnarled oaks are old, much older than they look—they bring to mind the centuries-old orchards of twisted olives in Tuscany. But no reds such as these ever lit up the valleys of Tuscany. On the distant horizon, the blue of the mountains curves up to the rim of the sky.

Finally, I turn back, descending Rabun Bald on the same trail by which I came.

Now the sun is approaching its zenith, sifting down through the leaves. I forget about being alone and am lost in the rapture of the golden foliage, the hickory leaves translucent in the sun. The woods seem a great cathedral, lit this Sunday morning just for me. A dome of light, tall columns of trees holding up the golden roof, a floor of gold and red, like a glorious Byzantine mosaic. Light pours down through the leaves, and I am baptized in glory streaming down from the heavens.

I think that perhaps this will be the last time I hike alone. Yet I do not feel alone. It is no longer a solitary climb but somehow a great losing of myself in something larger. I am lifted up in beauty.

—A. L.

OPPOSITE: *This image completes the trifecta of trees I painted at Rabun Bald. Here the trunks rising like columns lift up a dome of gold leaves, and the effect is like that of light pouring through a stained glass window. The viewpoint of the painting, looking up toward the sky beyond the trees, emphasizes the rise.*

Rabun Bald misses being the state's highest peak by eighty-eight feet. Its elevation of 4,696 feet is dwarfed only by that of Brasstown Bald about fifty miles to the west (chapter 26), also in the Chattahoochee National Forest.

Even so, nothing about Rabun Bald is second rate; naturalists, biologists, and everyday nature lovers tout the mountain as one of Georgia's most majestic natural areas. Many veteran hikers who have trekked all over Georgia's mountains say the most breathtaking views in the state are from the summit of Rabun Bald—even surpassing those from atop Brasstown Bald. On clear days the view from Rabun Bald may extend for more than one hundred miles into Georgia, North Carolina, and South Carolina, offering endless panoramic vistas of the rolling southern Appalachian Mountains. Wave after wave of gentle ridges and valleys, weathered by time, accentuate the region like a rumpled light blue blanket on an unmade bed.

While exploring this region—the Cherokee lands—in Georgia and the Carolinas in 1775, Bartram wrote of being enraptured and astonished by "a world of mountains piled upon mountains." His progress, he said, "was rendered delightful by the sylvan elegance of the groves, cheerful meadows, and high distant forests, which in grand order presented themselves to view."

As he ascended a peak in Georgia, Bartram came across a beautiful flowering tree "growing in a high degree of perfection." He determined that it probably was a species of magnolia but one that he'd never seen before. He was so impressed by the tree that he named the peak Mount Magnolia. Later, the peak came to be known as Rabun Bald. Although Bartram had discovered a new species, he waited sixteen years to publish an account of it. In the meantime, the British nurseryman John Fraser had come to America and collected a specimen of the tree from northwestern South Carolina in 1787. A botanical book published the following year credited Fraser with finding the new magnolia. Although Bartram is recognized today as the true discoverer of the tree, the species is known as the Fraser magnolia—a beautiful tree growing as high as forty feet and producing large, showy white flowers. It typically grows on moist slopes of the Appalachians at elevations of two thousand to four thousand feet.

Inspired by Bartram's travels, the Bartram Trail now allows thousands of hikers to roughly retrace his footsteps. The 115-mile trail winds from the North Georgia mountains into North Carolina.

A moderate, 1.8-mile segment of the Bartram Trail leads to Rabun Bald's summit. Numerous visitors who have made the trek to the top say they have experienced Bartram's feeling of awe and wonder during their ascent. For one thing, the Rabun Bald area rates among Georgia's leading botanical sites, according to the Georgia Botanical Society. Along the way to the summit, ferns unfurl and wildflowers add bright color. In some stretches, dense growths of mountain laurel, rosebay rhododendron, and Catawba rhododendron intertwine and turn the trail into a dark green tunnel. Hardy, gnarled oaks just off the trail have been dated to the 1730s, perhaps seen by Bartram himself.

A rich cove forest containing abundant spring ephemeral wildflowers surrounds the high rocky summit. The summit area also harbors many high-elevation plants, including mountain fetterbush, rock harlequin, and various shades of red trillium (also known as wake robin). In addition, several tree species more characteristic of northern forests and higher elevations are found here, including black chokeberry and American mountain ash (the latter produces striking clusters of red berries in the fall). Near the summit is a zone of dwarf oak heath, mainly scarlet oak and purple rhododendron.

Over the years, biologists have documented dozens of species at Rabun Bald that are rare elsewhere in Georgia. Some, such as wretched sedge, granite dome goldenrod, and rock gnome lichen, grow nowhere in the world except the southern Appalachians. In recent years, a new species of moss was discovered on Rabun Bald and in nearby North Carolina. Scientists named it Rabun Bald feather moss.

At the very top, common ravens—solid black, crow-size birds—often soar playfully above and around the observation platform as they pass in and out of forests that were never logged. The dark birds lend a certain charm and air of mystery to the mountain. Adding to the aura is an enduring Native American legend that says that Rabun Bald also is inhabited by fire-breathing demons who guard sacred caves and strange stone cairns hidden in the forest.

Regardless, ordinary folks who make it to Rabun Bald's top are sure to find serenity and one of the grandest views of natural splendor in all of Georgia.

—C. S.

28 The Pocket at Pigeon Mountain

Georgia's most spectacular wildflower destination

In circles of wildflower enthusiasts, the online world resounds each spring with praises of the Shirley Miller Wildflower Trail. If wildflower lovers in Georgia have a mecca, it is this mile-long trail tucked into the arms of Pigeon Mountain in the northwest corner of the state, in a cove known as "the Pocket."

What justifies the acclamations? I set out one April Saturday to see for myself.

The road from Atlanta wound north through the town of Lafayette and then on to the colorfully named Hog Jowl Road. A sign soon pointed to the turnoff for the Shirley Miller Wildflower Trail, a rough dirt lane ending at the parking lot for the trailhead. Here, an excited buzz of voices displaced the morning quiet. Scores of people were gathered among the cars, talking and gesturing with animation.

Apparently, more than one large group of wildflower enthusiasts had arrived. The Georgia Native Plant Society was here for its annual pilgrimage, the field trip I had planned to join. But the Georgia Botanical Society was here as well, for a talk by Leslie Edwards: speaker, educator, and lead author of the comprehensive reference *Natural Communities of Georgia.* I was thrilled. That book had been the primary text for my master naturalist class.

The leaders pulled together, seemingly conferring. As their members milled around, I heard behind me the voice of Charlie Seabrook and turned to see the man whose bucket list had brought me here. A born storyteller, his arms were outstretched as he waxed eloquently before the small group gathered around him.

I laughed. On this day, this small dirt parking lot was a veritable who's who of the Georgia botanical world.

The leaders addressed the general membership. The leaders for the two groups would alternate, giving everyone a double helping of education.

The Georgia Native Wildflower group would begin with an improvised exploration of the streamside trail across the parking lot from the Wildflower Trail. I followed: the spring blooms of the Shirley Miller Trail would have to wait just a bit longer.

Our guide, a young doctoral candidate named Troy, was indeed adept at identifying the beautiful wildflowers that spread a delicate carpet of color across the forest floor. But he confessed his real expertise was the world of amphibians—salamanders and newts. Aware that our next leg would be led by Leslie, a botanist, our group agreed to explore the stream for some field zoology.

Like kids, we plunged our hands into the water, teetering on slippery steppingstones to turn over rocks and sift through gravel to uncover the small critters inhabiting this clear mountain stream. From salamanders to mud puppies, we fished out the strange incarnations of the amphibian world, presenting them to Troy in our cupped hands for identification and enlightenment. Troy explained that the Southeast is a global hot spot for salamanders and newts: when the glaciers of the ice ages marched down the continent, they wiped out these warm climate species in much of North America but

OPPOSITE: *Sweeping brushstrokes create the layered rocks around the Pocket Falls at the end of the Shirley Miller Wildflower Trail. The procession of trees leaning into the picture, the angles of the cliff face, and the stairsteps of the mountain stream all conspire to pull the viewer into the painting and toward the falls, much like the inexorable pull I felt while walking the trail.*

The perfect form of the golden celandine poppy is thrown into sharp relief by the shadows behind it. The surrounding bluebells play accompaniment in simple but carefully rendered lines over transparent blue washes. A field of green conveys the rich underlayer of foliage below the flowers without distracting from their beautiful shapes.

stopped just short of the Southeast, leaving it with one of the most abundant amphibian populations in the world.

A patterned rock in the water demanded a closer look. I held it out to Troy, who announced it was a fossilized coral bud—sixty million years old or more. Here in the foothills of the Appalachian Mountains was a relic of the seabeds that once covered this part of the continent.

My cup was overflowing, but now it was time for the reason I had come—the Shirley Miller Wildflower Trail.

Leslie led us to the first section of the trail, a raised boardwalk built to protect the flowers from the feet of their spring admirers. On either side of the walk, waving and dancing on raised stems, was a kaleidoscope of color, an abundance of flowers the likes of which I had never seen in the wild. The entire bottomland was a forest meadow of bluebells and yellow poppies.

Nowhere else in Georgia can you see this profusion of bluebells and native celandine poppies. Leslie explained the unique conditions that create this oasis of northerly wildflowers. The waters of Pigeon Creek and the north-facing slope of Pigeon Mountain together form a cool moist microclimate that shelters these flowers of more northern climes, species prevalent here when the ice ages reigned. Their array is a living memory tended entirely by nature.

April had ushered out the first flush of bloodroot and liverwort; the trout lilies were mostly long gone. But as we ambled along the boardwalk and then along the more rustic path beside the stream, we enjoyed the fullness of spring's gifts. Magically, purple phacelia sprouted directly from the rocks along the stream. Wild pink geranium, so delicate and different from the nursery staple of the same name (no relation), toothworts and foamflowers, phlox and trillium, red columbine nodding—every wildflower in the East seemed to be here in some measure.

As we reached the beginning of the boardwalk and gathered to listen to Leslie, a strange winged creature darted and hovered among the bluebells. It almost appeared to be the shimmer of a hummingbird, with its marks of red and green.

Electrified, Leslie pointed and said, "Look! A hummer moth!"

It was the flower's natural pollinator. I raised my camera to snap the photo, the moment captured.

—A. L.

The great white trillium emerges almost imperceptibly from the white of the paper, one of thousands of bent trilliums that appeared like glowing apparitions along the hill by the trail. The diminutive blossoms of twoleaf miterwort make a curtain of spangled streamers that part before the majestic face of the trillium.

This painting captures the sheer conviviality of the trail's wildflowers as they jostle and nod to one another across the forest floor, as though meeting for a great celebratory spring social. Wild geranium and liverwort blossoms greet one another amid a jumble of new leaves.

In several areas of northwest Georgia's mountains, ideal combinations of geology, microclimate, and water create biologically splendid habitats that, in early spring, teem with an amazing diversity of wildflowers. Of these places, the best known by far is the Pocket of Pigeon Mountain in Walker County—a part of the rugged mountainous region known as the Appalachian Plateau in Georgia's northwest corner.

Many plant enthusiasts tout the Pocket as the most spectacular site for spring wildflowers in Georgia. "A few other sites come close, but none pack such a great diversity of plant species in such a compact area, and that's especially so with plants rare to Georgia, including some that are only found at this one location," said Richard Ware, a former president of the Georgia Botanical Society.

Geologically, the Pocket is a narrow valley—or a miniature gorge—bordered by steep slopes and limestone cliffs. The slopes and valley floor support what botanists say is an outstanding example of a mesic hardwood forest. Such forests are admired for their lushness, biological diversity, and beauty, particularly in early spring when their wildflowers burst into riots of blooms. The forests occur where soil on the valley floor is deep and rich in a cool moist environment. The dominant tree species is the tulip tree, also known as tulip poplar. Other "indicator species" (indicators of a healthy environment) are American beech, northern red oak, yellow buckeye, and southern sugar maple.

On the Pocket's floor, the deep fertile soil is composed of rich sediments and rocky detritus washed down by rain from the slopes and cliffs. Included in the mix is calcium from the limestone, which renders the soil neutral, or nearly neutral, rather than acidic. Many early spring wildflowers thrive best in neutral soils. Pocket Branch, a small swift stream that runs through the Pocket, helps to maintain the soil moisture levels crucial for plant growth. Occasionally, the stream overflows and deposits fertile alluvial matter—clay, sand, and silt—on the Pocket's floor.

Contributing to the natural richness are the Pocket's slopes, particularly those facing north. North-facing slopes usually are cooler and moister than south-facing slopes. That's because north-facing slopes receive less sunlight because of their position relative to the sun. Less sunlight also means less evaporation, making north-facing slopes more moist. The result is a cooler, wetter "microclimate" highly favorable to wildflowers.

These elements together make the Pocket one of the most remarkable natural treasures in the Southeast—a botanical wonderland. In addition to the trees, dozens of species of wildflowers, flowering shrubs, and woody vines flourish here—including ten species found only in a few other places in Georgia, such as celandine poppy, Ohio buckeye, bent trillium, lanceleaf trillium, wild hyacinth, log fern, harbinger of spring (a member of the parsley family), Virginia bluebells, hairy (or hoary) mock orange, and blue ash.

This great gift from nature is what draws throngs of visitors to the Pocket each spring. They come to see the lush growths of spring ephemerals and other early spring wildflowers in a sea of color. The ephemerals are short-lived wildflowers that emerge from dormancy in March and April and bloom for a few weeks. They include trout lilies, bloodroot, toothwort, harbinger of spring, squirrel corn, blue cohosh, twinleaf, Virginia bluebell, Dutchman's breeches, spring beauty, wood anemone, windflower, bleeding heart, bluets, and some trilliums. They bloom early by taking advantage of the sun that shines through the still-leafless trees and warms the soil. After blooming, the ephemerals quickly make fruit and set seed, then die back to their underground parts by late May. By summer, finding evidence that they ever existed is nearly impossible. But when they are in full bloom, they are some of nature's most glorious sights, superb delights to artists and photographers.

The Pocket's other spring wildflowers are just as beautiful, but botanists don't consider them ephemerals. These include most trillium species, violets, jack-in-the-pulpit, wild ginger, hepatica, rue anemone, and many others. Their blooms are also short-lived, but their stems and leaves may persist—unlike those of spring ephemerals—through much of summer.

When in bloom, most, if not all, of these magnificent wildflowers pop up along the Shirley Miller Wildflower Trail, which runs for nearly a half-mile through the Pocket. A wooden boardwalk protects its first eight hundred feet or so, taking visitors across the Pocket's most sensitive areas. The rest of the trail is a rugged, somewhat difficult footpath—also bordered by a profusion of spring blooms—that goes to the base of the breathtaking Pocket Waterfall, which feeds the creek. Whether on the boardwalk or footpath, one can hardly take a step without encountering several blooming wildflowers vying for space.

More than half a century ago, though, few if any visitors came to the Pocket. Few people outside a tight circle of botanists and other plant enthusiasts knew about it. In 1969 Georgia began leasing a huge swath of Pigeon Mountain to protect its natural features, including weird rock formations (Rock Town), some of the nation's deepest caves (Ellison and Pettyjohn caves), and the wildflower sanctuary called the Pocket. Several years later, at the urging of then-governor Jimmy Carter, the state Department of Natural Resources (DNR) bought more than thirteen thousand acres of the highly desirable landscape. It was named the Crockford-Pigeon Mountain Wildlife Management Area in honor of the late Jack Crockford, the director of Georgia's Fish and Game Commission in the late 1970s. The purchases included the Pocket in Pigeon Mountain's northwestern section. Word spread fast among nature lovers that the amazing wildflower habitat was now publicly owned. The Pocket quickly became the destination for legions of wildflower lovers in spring. Then, just as quickly, it became overwhelmed with people trampling the colorful blooms and compacting the fertile soil.

Concerned that the Pocket would be ruined, the DNR decided to build the boardwalk, which opened to the public in 1998. "We developed the boardwalk because people were going there to see the flowers, but they were loving them to death by walking around all in there and actually stepping on them," said David Gregory, a wildlife biologist with the DNR. "So, to protect the flowers, we built the boardwalk."

The agency named it for Shirley Miller, who was married to Zell Miller, then Georgia's governor. She was instrumental, the DNR said, in urging her husband to secure funding for the boardwalk and trail and, later, to designate the Pocket as one of Georgia's natural heritage preserves.

—C. S.

29 Rocktown

A maze of house-size boulders, textured walls, and stairstep climbs

Halfway up the mile-long trail to Rocktown, the first large boulder comes into view, an alien presence on the peaceful slope of the mountain, a beast of massive bulk milling among the trees.

It's late fall, and I'm hiking the Rocktown Trail on Pigeon Mountain in northwest Georgia's Walker County. I've come with my niece, Megan, who is visiting on Thanksgiving break from her junior year at college. I find Megan a friendly but slightly intimidating presence, a tall young woman with a long list of talents from surfing to softball to ballet.

I'm grateful to have this interesting Georgia wonder to share with my adventurous young relative.

On the drive to Pigeon Mountain, Megan read aloud Charlie Seabrook's description of Rocktown, enthusiastically sharing additional snippets from a search on her phone. Rocktown is a collection of house-sized boulders on Pigeon Mountain's ridgeline, she related, with textured formations that seem tailor-made for climbing. The tops of some rocks afford views that stretch for miles.

Hiking another ten minutes brings us to the top of the mountain, where the trail devolves into a maze of paths between towering boulders. The sprawling formation does have the feel of a town—perhaps one from

OPPOSITE: *Huge boulders form a labyrinth of town-like alleys at Rocktown on Pigeon Mountain. Here, I softened the background to emphasize the beautiful crisp edges of tree shadows on the rock—multihued blues bleeding into the aquamarine lichens on the adjoining rock. Its surface exhibits the knobby texture known as turtleback.*

medieval times with little back streets and alleys too narrow to admit more than a small cart. We follow the passages, turning first one way and then another. A renegade tree here or there has thrust up between the rocks.

The surfaces of the boulders are a wonderment—none smooth, almost all broken and pocked with odd protrusions and crevices.

Megan notices everything. She stops at one cliff-like formation to ask what causes the concentric rings of rock rippling across its side. I shake my head and wish I knew. Another boulder presents curled outer layers like peeling bark, petrified in stone.

Before long we encounter a boulder studded with ledges and handholds, its slope an irresistible invitation for climbing. Grasping at rocky knobs and wedging my feet into crevices, I'm excited to find myself easily scaling the huge rock right alongside my niece.

At the top, forty feet in the air, we can see all the way down the mountain. The far horizon is blue with more mountains. Nearer at hand are many more boulders scattered down the mountainside. We clamber down to explore some more. We pass a few small groups of explorers. Some seem officially engaged in real climbing, or bouldering, as the sport is known when no special equipment is required. We watch an instructor help a young climber navigate an undercut on one of the more challenging rocks.

At the top of another huge boulder, we find the surface erupting in bumps like reptilian skin—I recall that these are called turtlebacks. We step carefully across a deep crevice to another high outcrop, this one carpeted in silver-blue lichen. Its snowflake tendrils intertwine with pincushions of bright moss, all against a background of fallen leaves, red with pink undersides and rippled outlines—maybe some sort of chestnut oak? I wonder. It's a glorious patchwork, stitched with threads of silver twigs and fallen brown needles.

We walk on. Every turn between the rocks yields a new view—a mountain vista, a deep crevice, an alley leading to an open glade.

Late afternoon brings long blue shadows crawling across the mountain. A thick layer of leaves has buried any sign of the trail that takes us back down the mountain. A trace of panic twinges in my gut.

In the end, Megan recognizes the first rock we passed at the top of the trail. We make our way back down the mountain at a leisurely stroll, with time for me to hear about her dreams for the future. Megan is majoring in civil engineering with a minor in hydrology. She says she wants to work on cleaning up polluted industrial sites and to help write environmental policy that improves the world.

I share the dream that has brought me here—to create paintings that let people see Georgia's beauty. I nurture the hope that my project will raise awareness, maybe even inspire some to act, to ensure a future for these special places.

Megan smiles and nods with enthusiasm, and I feel as if I have passed a torch from one generation to the next.

—A. L.

One of Rocktown's signature formations appears here, the Champagne Glass, which rises between two large boulders and is surrounded by trees. I simplified the palette to two colors, blue and warm brown, so the viewer could focus on the dizzying play of light and shadow found in Rocktown's passages. In this way the painting mimics the disorientation I felt while wandering among the rocks.

With its more than one hundred acres of massive boulders carved into an amazing array of bizarre shapes, Rocktown looks like nature's sculpture gallery. It is, in essence, a sprawling rock outcropping atop Pigeon Mountain in Georgia's Appalachian Plateau. Its labyrinth of huge rocks, some the size of three-story buildings, were sculpted into their weird forms across tens of millions of years by the forces of nature.

Rocktown, however, is not to be confused with its famous touristy cousin, Rock City, which is about thirty-five miles north atop Lookout Mountain near Chattanooga. Like Rocktown, the main draw of Rock City is its striking rock formations, but its owners carefully groomed it into a major tourist attraction decades ago, and it now draws tens of thousands of visitors each year from around the world. Its famous SEE ROCK CITY signs, painted on barn roofs and splashed across huge billboards, once were common along highways in the rural South.

Rocktown, on the other hand, is a natural area, untouched by development—owned and managed by the Georgia Department of Natural Resources as part of the Crockford-Pigeon Mountain Wildlife Management Area. Although its ancient rock formations are as enchanting as those of its tourist-luring cousin, Rocktown was for a long time little known among the general public. Perhaps a reason was that it once was a tightly held secret among locals and a small circle of rock-climbing enthusiasts. But in recent years it has become popular among outdoor enthusiasts and casual visitors who come to see the incredibly shaped rocks—minus the trappings of a tourist resort.

The relatively flat top of the Appalachian Plateau is sandstone. Although it is harder than limestone or shale, wind and water have nevertheless carved and sculpted it for millions of years. Sandstone's tendency to fracture into squarish blocks has made it vulnerable to weathering into the fantastic boulder formations at Rocktown. Some boulders are as large as a house, and the narrow alleyways between them give the impression that they form a town.

Every boulder has its unique features. Sauntering among the big rocks, visitors' imaginations may run wild as they see various forms in the boulders. One boulder that is twenty-five feet high is called the Champagne Glass because of its distinctive shape—a narrow pedestal supporting a caprock. A house-size boulder resembles the Great Sphinx of Giza in the Egyptian desert. Natural markings on the surfaces of some of the surrounding rocks even resemble hieroglyphics. One boulder looks like the profile of a bulldog. Some huge rock overhangs seem to defy gravity.

Several other big boulders perch precariously on one another and seem as if they could topple over at any moment. Many large boulders have peculiar weathering patterns that resemble turtle shells. Deep inside a narrow dark crevice of one of the massive rocks, visitors can see their breath even though the outside temperature may be close to 80 degrees Fahrenheit.

The vegetation adds to the picturesque scene. Dry crevices and shallow ledges in the rocks provide footings for stunted red maples, Virginia pines, black birches, rock chestnut oaks, rhododendrons, sparkleberry, mountain laurel, fringe tree, bush honeysuckle, Carolina jasmine, and numerous grasses and wildflowers. Moist rock walls support jack-in-the-pulpit, alumroot, and early saxifrage. Catawba rhododendron blooms beautifully in midspring.

In recent decades, Rocktown has become one of the most diverse bouldering destinations in the South. On any fair-weather day, one can expect to see several rock climbers crawling on, clambering over, or precariously clinging to some of the more challenging big boulders. The climbers use the small crevices, pits, slots, and other natural features in the rocks as footholds and handholds to make their ascents.

But enjoying the incredible rock formations that Rocktown has to offer does not require rock climbing. A trail, though not well defined, takes visitors on a two-mile walk around and among the scores of odd-shaped rocks. Exploring the massive boulders could consume the better part of a day. A common mistake of visitors is not allowing enough time to see this unusual place. But be forewarned: those who visit Rocktown are soon under its spell and may find themselves returning again and again.

—C. S.

30 McLemore Cove

Georgia's most picturesque mountain valley

"They were going to put a chicken plant right across the road."

Tori Phillips stands with Charlie Seabrook and me in the parking lot outside her business, a warehouse for textbooks and other educational materials. She gestures to the field across the road. "I thought if anyone was going to stop it, it would have to be me."

Tori is vice president of the McLemore Cove Preservation Society. When I called the nonprofit group for points of interest around the cove, Tori immediately called me back and volunteered to show us around. She produces a photocopied map of the cove marked with the loop of roads we will drive today. Our first stop is Cove Methodist Church, built in 1894. Mindful of my request for points of natural beauty, Tori says the views there are lovely. Charlie nods; he says he remembers this tiny historic building.

Charlie and I have been working on our book for more than a year, but this trip to McLemore Cove is our first Georgia wonder trip together. On the drive north from Atlanta, we talked nonstop. I learned about Charlie's life as a newspaper journalist, his decision not to accept admission to medical school, and his life philosophy in general, which includes "Be kind" and "Be curious." It seems to me that Charlie is curious about most things. He says he first discovered McLemore Cove in the summer of 1996—it appeared to

him a wonder, an enclave of historic farms, mountain views, springs and caves, birds and wildlife all mixed together, preserved somehow from the insatiable appetite of developers to the south.

Now it's almost twenty years later, and I wonder what we will find today.

We are visiting just after Memorial Day weekend. It's been a long cool spring, and the greens are vivid. Across the fields we spy rambling farmsteads—old frame houses huddled with wooden barns and outbuildings. Tori talks about the pressures of development and the struggles of the society to preserve the historic character of the family farms and community. Tori and other society members eventually were successful in staving off the chicken plant that was proposed in 2018. But she says the pressure never lets up. Lots of fancy new homes have sprung up in the cove, she says, pointing to their alien shapes among the older houses and farms.

We arrive at Cove Methodist Church, a tiny white frame structure with a steeple that plays hide-and-seek against the clouds scattered on the blue sky. Across the road is yet another old farm, its metal-roofed barns and silos shining silver against the green of Pigeon Mountain behind them. Pigeon Mountain frames the eastern border of McLemore Cove, which cuts a deep V fifteen miles long that opens to the north. The long ridge of Lookout Mountain forms its border to the west. Thus barricaded on either side, the cove has been somewhat protected from the ravening monster of Atlanta growth.

Despite the map, I lose track of exactly where we are. We ramble past the Martin Davis home and its outbuildings full of antiques. Charlie is eager to explore, but the gates are closed. Perhaps we can stop by later.

Tori takes us to a high hill on which the huge white barn of Mountain Cove Farms sits like a king, surveying the broad gold- and green-striped hayfields below. Bright purple thistles rise out of the high grass around the

OPPOSITE: *A fall visit to McLemore Cove yielded this spectacular view from the peak of Lookout Mountain in the Zahnd Wildlife Management Area. Brilliant red and copper trees frame the soft golds of the autumn fields a thousand feet below, flowing away to a blue horizon like a wide golden river.*

The goldfinch shines bright in the thistles above McLemore Cove's rolling fields. Mindful that a goldfinch on thistles is almost a visual cliché, I muted its outline so the viewer sees first the vivid purple flower, then finds the form of the bird against the sunlit field. In the distance, the blues of the mountains are the constant in the cove's ever-changing panorama.

barn, beacons for butterflies and a pair of bright goldfinches. The farm is part of a two-thousand-acre wildlife corridor purchased by the Georgia Department of Natural Resources and Walker County to link Zahnd Natural Area on Lookout Mountain with the Crockford-Pigeon Mountain Wildlife Management Area just across the cove. The incredible diversity of wildlife in McLemore is partly the result of its location in this transition zone between the Appalachian Plateau and the Valley and Ridge Region of the Georgia Appalachians.

We finish with a visit to the family farm of Tori's husband, which she says is typical of the cove's old homesteads. Against a hill behind the house, a mountain-fed spring becomes a clear creek, tumbling over a low wall—an old mill dam—to meander its way across a green field. Small rocks glow red and gold in the clear water, and a multitude of tiny black snails dot the rocks. Wild hydrangea, all in bloom, clambers around the banks of the spring, and a green anole scampers away as we approach this thriving habitat.

It's not a tourist attraction; it's off the beaten path. Yet this farm seems a fitting representative of a way of life that lingers here, just one gem in a necklace of jewels tucked into this natural wonder, a mountain cove steeped in the magic of another time.

—A. L.

McLemore Cove in northwest Georgia is without question one of the Southeast's most picturesque mountain valleys. Nestled between the steep slopes of Pigeon Mountain and Lookout Mountain, the cove is one of the most intact rural landscapes remaining in Georgia. Its pastoral countryside encompasses historic farmsteads, tree-shaded lanes, old barns, wooden fences, and gently rolling pastureland. Because of the limey soil, sweetly fragrant red cedar trees abound there—perhaps the greatest concentration of the evergreens in such a small area of Georgia. On each side of the cove, the steep limestone and sandstone walls of the mountains drop one thousand feet or more to the valley floor and form dramatic backdrops.

All this evokes a feeling of order, the neatness and efficiency of a mountain agricultural community in the late nineteenth and early twentieth centuries. A sense of history also pervades the area because of events that occurred there, especially the bloody Battle of Chickamauga (which took place a few miles north of the cove).

The cove's engrossing history, idyllic landscape, and natural beauty led to designation of its entire fifty thousand acres as a historic district in 1994 and its listing on the National Register of Historic Places.

Historic preservationists take great delight in McLemore Cove, but wildlife biologists and conservationists regard it as a marvel of nature, one of Georgia's most valuable natural assets. Conservationists have called the cove and its surrounding mountainous terrain a "unique and biologically diverse" area with "extraordinary wildlife habitat."

For that reason, the Georgia Department of Natural Resources, with help from land preservation groups and others, vigorously pursued efforts to purchase a large swath of McLemore Cove and permanently protect its ecological riches. In 2008 the state and its conservation partners, including Walker County, acquired 1,840 acres consisting of a ridge, mountain slopes, and bottomland in the cove—all ecologically significant. In addition, several owners of large adjacent tracts, totaling twenty-two hundred acres of mostly forested wildlife habitat, protected their properties through conservation easements. In all, the state and its partners spent about $11 million to preserve McLemore Cove's natural riches for future generations.

The protected property today provides diverse habitats—hardwood- and pine-dominated forests, sandstone outcrops, caves, springs, and open pastureland—that harbor rare species such as the green salamander, Barksdale trillium, and Georgian cave beetle. The high degree of diversity is a result of McLemore Cove's topography and unique location between Pigeon Mountain to the east and Lookout Mountain to the west. At the head of the valley, the mountains join at a juncture that is part of the transition zone between two of Georgia's five physiogeographic regions—the Appalachian Plateau and the Ridge and Valley Regions.

At the juncture, the cove's protected wildlands create a corridor for wildlife and human recreation by linking two other important publicly owned tracts, the Crockford-Pigeon Mountain Wildlife Management Area on Pigeon Mountain and the Zahnd Wildlife Management Area atop Lookout Mountain—twenty thousand acres in all. Both WMAs descend from their mountain summits to the floor of McLemore Cove nearly one thousand feet below. From overlooks atop each mountain, magnificent views of the cove can leave one breathless.

The sandstone topping the two mountains allows water to seep downward through cracks and ravines, dissolving the underlying limestone layers and creating extensive cave systems. The water flows out at numerous springs at the bases of the mountains. The tops of both mountains also feature "rock towns," or sites with large boulders molded eons ago by geologic forces into all kinds of weird shapes and sizes (see chapter 29).

The cove itself was named for the brothers John and Robert McLemore, early settlers who were sons of a Scottish trader and a Cherokee mother. For centuries before European settlers arrived, Cherokee and Creek peoples had occupied the area and were still living there when settlers started trickling in. A number of Indian trails ran through the cove and extended into present-day Alabama and Tennessee. Georgia and federal authorities, however, eventually brutally forced the native peoples out of their homeland and moved them west during the infamous Trail of Tears in 1838. The government used a land lottery to distribute most of the seized land, including McLemore Cove, to white citizens and veterans of the American Revolution, the War of 1812, and the Indian Wars.

Historically, however, McLemore Cove is perhaps best known for its role in the Civil War. In September 1863, the cove was the site of an encampment of fifteen thousand U.S. Army soldiers. Confederate forces then tried to use the V-shaped cove to hem in the Union troops and defeat them in what the rebels expected to be an overwhelming victory. But a series of Confederate mistakes allowed the U.S. Army to withdraw from the cove and move to the broader Chickamauga valley outside the cove. Shortly thereafter, the two armies faced each other at Chickamauga, which became the second-bloodiest battle of the Civil War, second only to the Battle of Gettysburg earlier the same year.

Today, McLemore Cove is a picture of peace and serenity. The natural splendor, rural solitude—and human history—make it one of the most rewarding places to visit in Georgia.

—C. S.

31 The Chattooga River

Flowing wild and unimpeded through a temperate rainforest

We strapped on our helmets and signed the waivers. Two pages of fine print listed the ways in which we could be maimed, disabled, or drowned while whitewater rafting on the world-class rapids of the Chattooga River.

Three friends, Amy, Celeste, and Yasmin, had been game for the adventure.

We lined up with the other raft teams for the safety talk delivered by a strapping young fellow named Brandon, who turned out to be our guide. He issued a sobering list of instructions, including how to float—feet first—if we fell out of the raft. That way, he explained, we wouldn't get our head smashed into a rock as the river carried us downstream.

"With all the rains we've had," he continued, "we're in for a treat. The water is very high in section III, and we're going to see some world-class rapids and beautiful waterfalls. It ends with an amazing run, Bull Sluice. We won't know if we can take it until we get closer. Normally we only take more experienced rafters."

My friends and I glanced at each other and raised our eyebrows in synchrony—a shared admission that we might not make the cut.

"It's cloudy today," Brandon concluded. "But I think this is when the river is at its best, when it's gray and misty like this morning. You'll be able to see why the Chattooga is special—why it's called a temperate rainforest."

We climbed into the inflatable raft. Brandon pushed off and jumped in. The waters were turbulent, swollen with recent rains, and we were swept away on the powerful current.

Designated a National Wild and Scenic River, the Chattooga is protected from development for almost sixty miles. Unimpeded by dams, it batters rock and cliff in a crashing descent from its headwaters at Whitesides Mountain in North Carolina to Tugalo Lake in South Carolina, delineating the border between Georgia and South Carolina along the way. The drop of almost two thousand feet, through a rocky chasm, leaves little room for human encroachment.

We moved through untouched wilderness. Giant rocks loomed out of the water, evoking fallen monuments or the remains of ancient civilizations. Birds cried unseen from trees pressing the river in a wall of green. The pale blossoms of rhododendron shone through the gray mist. Rounding a bend, we were surprised by a high waterfall to one side, its long white fingers running down a cliff to the river.

Soon the river began to churn—we were approaching a run of rapids. Our raft bucked in the water, a bronco ready to unseat its riders. The atmosphere was charged, tense. "Get down," Brandon said as he steered us between boulders. We slid to sit on the bottom of the raft to lessen the chance of flipping. A fragment of instruction flashed through my mind—"keep your feet raised if you fall—a dangling foot can get trapped in a rock and pull you under." The river seemed unforgiving of strangers.

In a few minutes, the waters calmed. Brandon steered us to a sandy spot for a welcome lunch break. He unpacked our fare and spread it out on a huge rock. We ate and rested in the misty shadows of the trees as he shared more about this special place, his affection for the river obvious. The Chattooga watershed, he explained, captures warm wet air coming up from

OPPOSITE: *Gray mists made for our guide's favorite days on the Chattooga River. I minimized the color here, using glowing green for the rainforest moss and trees and stormy gray for the turbulent river. We encountered the huge leaning rock at the beginning of the journey; it looked like a fallen column at an ancient gate admitting us to the river wilderness. The faint silhouette of the raft in the background shows its diminutive size compared with the river.*

The waterfall and trees emerging from the mists of the Chattooga reminded me of the landscapes by the Chinese painter Li Tang, who painted during the Song Dynasty more than a thousand years ago. The two tiny figures huddled at the bottom of the falls, a photographer and a woman holding an umbrella, pay homage to his beautiful work Mountain Landscape with Two Men Looking at a Waterfall.

the Atlantic. The heavy load of water drops as rain when the air mass meets the high wall of the Blue Ridge escarpment. The resulting eighty inches of rainfall each year creates this temperate rainforest—one of the few east of the Mississippi, he said. The moist shady gorges of the Chattooga shelter plants found nowhere else—ferns and mosses that thrive in places that never dry out.

After lunch we resumed a peaceful paddle through a long quiet stretch of the river broken intermittently by runs of rapids. The voice of the river, wild and tumultuous, followed us throughout our journey.

Midafternoon had passed by the time we neared Bull Sluice. Brandon steered our raft to the riverbank. We watched him confer with other guides gathered with their groups.

"We won't be taking Bull Sluice today," he announced when he returned. "It's too wild. But we can watch a more advanced group take it."

I was both relieved and strangely disappointed.

We climbed out of the raft and scrambled to the highest rock to watch the more experienced rafters take the famous run. The river exploded in white spray, crashing through a narrow gap in the rocks. We watched it thrust and toss the boat like a toy into the churning waters below.

Rain clouds suddenly opened up. We were soaked, exhilarated, filled with wonder at the Chattooga's power and the beauty of this unexpected wild rainforest. As we drove home, we marveled at its contradictions—green quiet and explosive waters, mossy riverbanks and hard rock. We agreed that we were already feeling the loss of this strange and beautiful place.

And all of us vowed to come back to meet Bull Sluice another day.

—A. L.

In the late 1960s, it was becoming crystal clear to Congress and President Lyndon Johnson's administration that numerous American rivers were suffering horribly from decades of pollution, damming, and development. Some streams were so stagnant and dirty with industrial filth that they occasionally caught fire—most notably, the Cuyahoga River in Cleveland, Ohio.

In one of the most significant efforts to atone for the long-time neglect of the nation's waterways, Congress passed the 1968 National Wild and Scenic Rivers Act. The measure says, "It is hereby declared to be the policy of the United States that certain selected rivers of the Nation which, with their immediate environments, possess outstandingly remarkable scenic, recreational, geologic, fish and wildlife, historic, cultural or other similar values, shall be preserved in free-flowing condition, and that they and their immediate environments shall be protected for the benefit and enjoyment of present and future generations."

The rip-roaring, fifty-eight-mile Chattooga River, which flows along a segment of the eastern edge of northern Georgia, met those stringent requirements. After a strong push by powerful proponents of the river, including then-Georgia governor Jimmy Carter, Congress officially declared it a National Wild and Scenic River in May 1974. It was the first such designation for a river east of the Mississippi. Today the unspoiled Chattooga remains the only river in Georgia and South Carolina with that designation—and one of the longest and most spectacular free-flowing mountain rivers in the nation. Its protected river corridor encompasses gorges, cliffs, scenic waterfalls, and rich forests within more than fifteen thousand acres of three national forests—the Chattahoochee in Georgia; the Sumter in South Carolina; and the Nantahala in North Carolina.

The three states share the river. It originates as small rivulets, fed by springs and abundant rainfall, high in the Appalachian Mountains of western North Carolina. Bucking, churning, and thundering between stretches of calmness, the river runs its rugged course down into Georgia and South Carolina. A little more than seven miles of it are solely within Georgia; another forty-two miles form Georgia's border with South Carolina. Along the way, a section of the river flows through the Ellicott Rock Wilderness, which spans all three national forests and three states.

Numerous miles of moderate to challenging—and sometimes dangerous—hiking trails run parallel to the Chattooga. They provide breathtaking views of the roaring river and its amazing beauty and diverse flora and fauna. But to fully experience the river's raw power and glory, one must navigate it in a canoe, kayak, or raft—preferably a raft operated by an experienced commercial guide.

Watercraft-wise, the Chattooga is not a river for the faint of heart. When it reaches its terminus in quiet Tugalo Lake, a reservoir between Georgia and South Carolina, the river has dropped nearly a half-mile in elevation. The steep descent creates turbulent vortexes, hydraulics, thundering rapids, rock-strewn channels, and deep pools that challenge even the most skilled kayakers, canoeists, and rafters. Even so, it remains one of the nation's most popular white-water rivers. "Untold numbers and kinds of people have felt the river's torrents," John Lane writes in *Chattooga: Descending into the Myth of Deliverance River*.

For management purposes, the Chattooga's official watchdog (the U.S. Forest Service) divides the river into five sections, 0 through IV. Section 0 includes the river's headwaters, from its beginning on the slopes of the Appalachians in North Carolina to the Russell Bridge, where Georgia Highway 28 crosses the river. Sections I to IV cover the portions of the river open to boating, including the West Fork (section I) southward to section IV and the river's end at Tugalo Lake. Section I is slow and gentle, suitable for beginner canoeists. Section II includes shelf-like rapids and a rip-snorting Class III rapid popular with novice whitewater boaters and others. Section III requires considerable whitewater boating skill with roaring, violent rapids up to Class V. (Numerous boating fatalities have occurred on section III.) Section IV is the most treacherous and dangerous of the sections with numerous Class III, IV, and V rapids. The Forest Service warns that only expert boaters should attempt that section. Section IV ends as the river flows into Tugalo Lake.

Section IV was where the river segment of the critically acclaimed motion picture *Deliverance* was filmed. The movie is about four Atlanta businessmen who decide to canoe down a wild river in the remote

Georgia wilderness before the river is dammed—and they meet mayhem and mishaps along the way. The landmark film, which came out in July 1972, showed Americans the intense thrills (and danger) of white-water rafting. Even though the storyline made viewers uncomfortable, the film is credited with sparking a nationwide interest in whitewater boating. One also might say the movie meant deliverance for the river itself: it helped generate public support and political decisions that resulted in the Chattooga's designation as a National Wild and Scenic River—which granted it permanent protection.

—C. S.

32 Sosebee Cove

High-elevation, north-facing cove a rare treasury of plant and amphibian life

I planned my visit to Sosebee Cove in the Chattahoochee National Forest for early April, unsure of what I would find. The cove was said to be a botanical bonanza with, according to Charlie Seabrook, a "rich diversity of shade-tolerant trees, shrubs, and wildflowers."

The 175-acre cove in Union County is bisected by a winding mountain road that leads to the trailhead and a few parking spaces eked out of the mountainside. When I arrived, I found the trees overhead still bare, the forest floor brown with last year's fallen leaves. Had I come too early?

The trail led downslope to the lower section of the cove. The forest lay under a blanket of quiet, embroidered with the occasional ripple of birdsong. I thought of the warblers and redstarts that migrate through each spring on their way to nesting grounds in the North.

The air was moist. Along the trail, rivulets of spring streams gurgled between rocks nestled into crevices. A flicker of movement caught my eye—a salamander tail. I remembered that this north-facing slope, high in the mountains, is a haven for salamanders. Nearly every species in the Southeast can be found here, tucked into the cool damp spaces between rock and water.

As I made my way along the path, massive trunks of old trees rose up to greet me—tulip trees and the rarer yellow buckeyes standing among

An immense boulder and nearby tree dwarf the surrounding saplings and fill this early spring landscape at Sosebee Cove. Stippled ink creates the dense textures of the forest floor, while a bright wash of green becomes the mossy covering creeping over rocks and trees. A simple two-color palette allows the viewer to enjoy the subtle textures of rock, twig, and tree, so easy to miss once the forest cove is in full leaf.

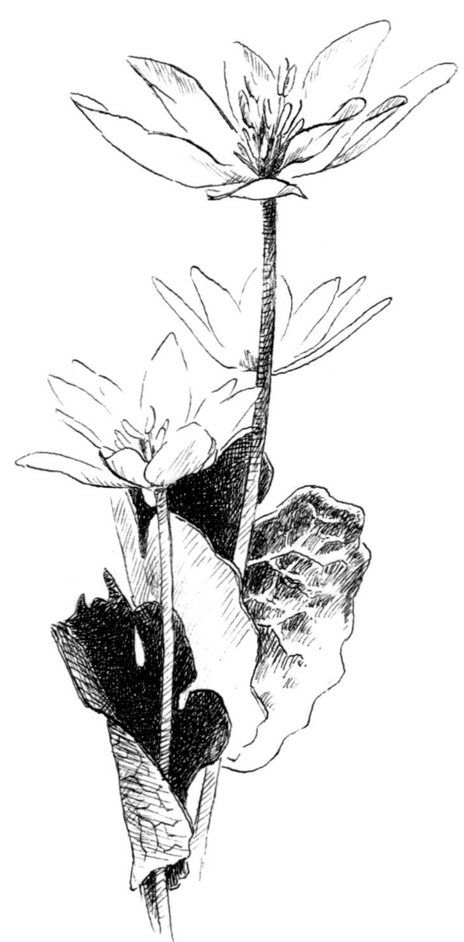

younger saplings. Huge boulders made a periodic appearance—outliers, no doubt, from the boulderfield above the road, the relic of a glacial age that broke the mountains through millennia of freezing and thawing.

To my delight, I began to spy small wildflowers at my feet. Here, high in the mountains, only the earliest flowers were in bloom. Red trillium, and spring beauty with fine lines of pink incised on its petals.

And, finally, the pure white blossoms of bloodroot, my favorite spring wildflower. No other blossom can match its white perfection, its symmetry. The flowers rose from the tattered remains of old leaves in pools of starry white, like bright constellations shining amid the dead dark matter of the old year. I stooped to inspect the beautiful flowers, newborn in a world just waking from winter's sleep.

Sosebee's miracle that day was not the gift of spring abundance, the profligate unfolding of all its wildflowers. Instead, it was its first perfection—the flowering of the bloodroot, that perfect harbinger of spring.

—A. L.

The flower called spring beauty thrusts its way past the dappled leaves of trout lily and a trident of toothwort leaves. The color is muted, to illuminate the glorious leaves: the ruffled toothwort and the mottled trout lily, their forms no less beautiful than the blossoms.

I thought of this as a Creation painting, life emerging in beautiful symmetry from the dead matter of the forest floor. The architectural lines of the drawing are deliberately exposed, suggesting the act of creation in progress.

The Southern Appalachian Mountains of North Georgia are dotted with picturesque mountain coves, basically small, V-shaped valleys between ridges closed at one or both ends. Growing within many of them are lush deciduous forests teeming with rich assortments of animals and shade-tolerant trees, shrubs, and wildflowers. These so-called rich cove forests—some of the nation's most diverse ecosystems—are unique to the Southern Appalachians.

Because of its superb beauty and diversity, the 175-acre, high-elevation Sosebee Cove is Georgia's most celebrated rich cove forest. Much of it was logged in the early 1900s, but its maturing second-growth forest today gives visitors the impression that they are in a swath of old growth.

A part of the rugged Blue Ridge region of the Chattahoochee National Forest, the cove is permanently protected as the Sosebee Cove Scenic Area and Trail. It's renowned for its large tulip trees and yellow buckeyes. The buckeyes are said to be the largest trees of their kind in the United States, having escaped logging because their wood was not profitable. Several are more than 175 years old. Just a few feet from the start of the half-mile trail through the cove is the moss-covered trunk of Georgia's largest yellow buckeye, which has a diameter of five feet. Equally impressive are the cove's tulip trees, which are said to be the best second-growth stand of their species in the nation.

The cove is home to many other tree species, including flowering dogwood, northern red oak, basswood, cucumber magnolia, white ash, southern sugar maple, ironwood, black cherry, and American beech.

A variety of natural conditions are responsible for Sosebee Cove's outstanding biodiversity. The cove is in an area of high rainfall. Its north-facing orientation and high elevation help keep it cool and moist even in droughts. Its dark nutrient-rich soil is deeply layered on the gentle concave slopes.

These conditions also make Sosebee Cove a refuge for plants that were forced farther south by advancing glaciers during the Pleistocene Epoch that ended about twelve thousand years ago. When the glaciers retreated, many of the plants remained, including trees such as black birch, striped and mountain maple, and the rare yellowwood tree.

Halfway along the cove's short trail, a big brown-and-white U.S. Forest Service sign proclaims that the cove is "a botanist's paradise." As if to prove that point, the cove abounds with seasonal wildflowers from spring through fall. In their book *Favorite Wildflower Walks in Georgia*, Hugh Nourse and Carol Nourse laud Sosebee Cove as one of the state's five top wildflower walks.

Among the more than two dozen spring-blooming flowers are bloodroot, giant chickweed, several trillium species, toothwort, mayapple, Dutchman's breeches, Jack-in-the-pulpit, showy orchid, bellwort, wild geranium, wood anemone, and umbrella leaf. Summer brings jewelweed, yellow wood sorrel, wood nettle, white snakeroot, skullcaps, Turk's-cap lily, and many more blooms. In late summer and fall come several species of sunflowers, goldenrods, and asters.

On the slopes are luxuriant growths of ferns—maidenhair, southern lady, marginal wood, hay-scented, and Christmas and cinnamon ferns, to name a few. Upslope on Sosebee Cove's northern side is an excellent example of a picturesque high-altitude boulderfield, which also offers a profusion of spring wildflowers, mosses, and ferns. The large angular boulders were apparently split by ice during the Pleistocene.

Spring bird watching in the cove can be superb. Commonly seen and heard there, beginning around late April, are American redstarts, rose-breasted grosbeaks, Kentucky warblers, hooded warblers, Blackburnian warblers, wood thrush, blue-headed vireos, and black-and-white warblers. Cove forests also are known for their exceptional variety of salamanders. More than twenty species of the moisture-loving amphibians live in the cove. They tend to take shelter beneath rotting logs and moss-covered rocks and in other secretive spots. Salamanders are quite sensitive to changes in the environment and thus serve as sentinels for the health of a forest.

One could not discuss Sosebee Cove, however, without mentioning the late Arthur Woody, the first U.S. Forest Service ranger in Georgia, who served from 1911 to 1945. Ranger Woody, the "barefoot ranger," loved this peaceful cove and negotiated its purchase by the Forest Service in 1925 from then-owner Alonzo Sosebee. Woody's efforts to preserve it as a natural area began in 1935 and culminated in its designation as the Sosebee Cove Scenic Area in September 1958. At that time Sosebee Cove also was dedicated as a memorial to Woody for his untiring work to preserve the beauty and great diversity of this magnificent place.

—C. S.

33 Cooper Creek Scenic Area

Home to large hemlocks, white pines, and Valley of the Giants

We followed the narrow road as it twisted up the mountain. The day was dark and misty. We'd been wandering this wild tract of North Georgia, part of the Chattahoochee National Forest, for more than an hour. Old logging roads branched off on either side of us and faded into the trees.

Were we lost? No. But we couldn't find what we were looking for: The Valley of the Giants.

We were in the Cooper Creek Scenic Area, which Charlie Seabrook described as harboring "large hemlocks and white pines, some with bases as big as four feet in diameter." When I went online to read more, I found myself especially captivated by the name of a destination within the scenic area: The Valley of the Giants, described by one website, sherpaguides.com, as a place where ancient tulip polars still live, with trunks as big as nineteen feet in circumference.

I had already come to this remote mountain wilderness twice in search of the giants, looking unsuccessfully for the unmarked trail.

Today my son Tyler, twenty-seven, had come with me, promising to help. He checked the printed directions again, from Sherpa Guides: "The trail pitches steeply north."

We crept past another old logging road barred with a metal gate. We'd passed it twice already, dismissing it because of its level grade – no "pitch" about it. But it did seem to be in the right general area.

Tyler pulled our car to the narrow shoulder and we got out, trying to decide whether to venture this dubious path. As we hesitated, a small hatchback pulled up behind us. A nondescript man, seeming neither young nor old, got out. He smiled and pulled out some hiking poles.

"Excuse me," I said. "Do you know if this is anywhere close to the Valley of the Giants?"

"Yes," he said, "this is the trail." He pointed to the old gated road.

I was elated. We'd found it!

He smiled. "It's only a mile or so to the trees."

At long last, I was finally going to see them—the mountain giants. Their trunks like huge columns, somehow still standing after two centuries of logging.

Tyler and I set out, the hiker ahead soon disappearing in the mist. Damp leaves muffled our footsteps; moss stretched its long green fingers over every rock and fallen log.

Within a half-mile we came to the crossing of Turkey Creek and we saw the first landmark—a green sunlit field across the creek, a bottomland that my map said had been in human cultivation since before white settlers arrived. My imagination painted Native American women tending mounds of squash or corn, nearby a cluster of boys knocking around a ball or playing a game.

We followed the trail as it turned away from the light-filled vista and into the shadowy forest.

White trilliums raised ghostly faces from the forest floor. A small dusky salamander scrambled beneath a leaf at our feet. Soon we became aware of the first silhouettes of the giants looming in the mist on the slopes above

OPPOSITE: *In this painting, I made the tree the hero, placing it large and in the center to mimic the hiker's experience of encountering its massive bulk along the trail in the Valley of the Giants at the Cooper Creek Scenic Area. The detailed focus on the pillowy moss emphasizes the rough textures of rock and bark. A mature tree on the right is included to convey the immense girth of the giant just beyond.*

the trail. We slowed and looked in wonder. The dwarfed the trees around them—trees that would be large in younger woods, but here they were lesser dwellers of an ancient place where giants live on. Moss shrouded the giants' massive bases in pillows of vivid green. I placed my hand on the trunk of one—how old? two hundred years? three hundred?

The hiker reappeared, perhaps returning from the trail's end.

"Should we go farther?" we asked.

"Yes," he said, "the biggest tree is just a little farther ahead. You'll see it on the left."

He was gone. I'd had this strange experience before: a feeling that each of these special places has a kind of guardian angel—someone who watches over it and guides friendly visitors along the path. Tyler and I remarked to each other on the man's face—bright eyes, unclouded by the troubles of the outside world, its passing stress and strains.

Tyler and I rested for long moments before we turned to hike back. Listening. The giants were silent, living in a different time, rooted in the mountain, to remain, l hoped, long after we had gone.

—A. L.

OPPOSITE: *Light and air open up from the top of this painting, highlighting a glimpse of the open bottomland just beyond Turkey Creek. Textured brush strokes grow thick toward the bottom of the picture, where lie the tattered remains of the previous year's growth. The shadowy darks make a dark frame for the spring green illuminating the distant meadow.*

Before the late 1800s, the virgin forests of North Georgia's majestic Appalachian Mountains were some of the planet's most magnificent natural systems. Gigantic chestnuts, oaks, cherries, ashes, walnuts, tulip poplars, hemlocks, beeches, and other trees hundreds of years old, twenty feet in circumference and 150 feet or more high, were common throughout the seemingly never-ending forests.

Then came northern industrial loggers. In a frenzied quest to fell vast sections of the virgin timber, they scooped up tens of thousands of acres of primeval forest from poor, uneducated mountain farmers and other landowners for as little as one dollar per acre. The loggers quickly set about felling the forests' incredibly huge trees. The prevailing logging method was "cut and leave," meaning that the companies had little desire to plant new trees or otherwise restore the land after the once-splendid forest was clear-cut and the landscape laid bare. The logging ruined pristine mountain streams. One historic account reports, "The loggers cut over the woods, took the big timber, butchered the woods."

Rapacious logging wasn't the only assault. Gold and coal mining, wildfires, overgrazing, and unregulated hunting and fishing also took heavy tolls on the forests. By the early 1900s, most of the once glorious mountain landscape had become so poor and depleted that nobody wanted it.

The federal government became alarmed, recognizing that an economic and natural catastrophe of huge proportions was in the making if the blighted land was not made whole again. In response, beginning in 1911, Congress authorized the U.S. Forest Service (created in 1905) to begin buying tens of thousands of acres of depleted mountain land. It proved to be a salvation. The forest was allowed to regenerate, aided by massive tree plantings in several areas. The work controlled soil erosion. The once nearly worthless land today makes up most of the 750,000-acre Chattahoochee National Forest, whose vast expanse now spreads across most of North Georgia. Nearly all of it is second- and third-growth forest that replaced the chopped-down virgin forest. Although the Forest Service has allowed some regulated logging to continue, the forest has regained much of its former beauty and biodiversity.

Remarkably, however, some swaths of the virgin Chattahoochee Forest and their humongous trees were never cut down. Somehow they escaped the deadly bites of axe and crosscut saw. As a result, they stand today as remnants of the original forest—hardy old-growth survivors of logging, disease, harsh weather, wildfires, and other adversities through the centuries. How they escaped being chopped down is, for the most part, a mystery. Luck no doubt played a role. Whatever the reason, we are fortunate today to have places like this one that inspire awe and remind us of how the forests once appeared—how Native Americans and early pioneers saw them—before massive destruction by loggers, miners, and other exploiters. "To ramble through these areas is to travel back in time, deep into how those woods looked without human interference," the retired Georgia forester Clifford Shaw writes in *Rambling through Old-Growth Forests Past and Present.*

The 1,240-acre Cooper Creek Scenic Area is one such place. It harbors what many consider the best example of the original forest that once graced North Georgia's mountains. It is surrounded by a larger forest unit, the thirty-one-thousand-acre Cooper Creek Wildlife Management Area, also part of the Chattahoochee National Forest. Hikers, botanists, and avid tree huggers make regular forays into the scenic area to study it and marvel at its amazingly huge trees, including the massive tulip poplars, "the finest old-growth tulip poplar trees in North Georgia," Shaw reports. In addition, he writes, the scenic area has the "finest surviving white oaks in the Chattahoochee National Forest." One is believed to be the second-largest white oak (thirteen feet in circumference and three hundred to four hundred years old) in the entire forest.

A trail, simply called the Old Growth Forest Hike, leads to most of these big trees. The first of them is several hundred yards from the start of the trail. Farther up are widely spaced specimens of large white and northern red oak and black birch. But the most impressive trees are the giant tulip poplars. Through the centuries storms have broken off the tops of many. While hikers can see many big trees from the trail, it's necessary to search for others above and below the path. The trail crosses a white pine ridge; about a quarter-mile farther on is the six-acre grove known as the Valley of the Giants, home to the largest poplars. At the trail's end is the giant of giants, a breathtaking tulip poplar nineteen feet in circumference.

It's hard to imagine that these majestic specimens also were once slated to become timber. Today they are permanently protected. While no one knows for sure why they escaped logging, their safeguarded status today is testament to one man's dogged determination and boundless love of Georgia's mountains.

He is the late Charles Wharton, still revered as one of the state's foremost naturalists. He walked Georgia's wilds tirelessly from mountain to sea and examined all that he found. In his monumental work, *The Natural Environments of Georgia*, he described one hundred of the state's natural habitats, from secluded mountain coves to sun-drenched coastal salt marshes. The book is still an essential guide for anyone—biologists, geologists, educators, land-use planners—studying Georgia's natural landscape. In the 1950s, he learned of stands of immensely huge trees in the Cooper Creek watershed of the Chattahoochee National Forest. He made his way there. As he later said, the sight of the gigantic old trees left him "profoundly incredulous." The place where they grew, he said, was perhaps "the last area of primeval forest in Georgia's mountains." Then he heard about something that shook him to the core—the Forest Service was planning to allow loggers to cut the trees down for timber.

He vowed that would not happen. Using every ounce of persuasive power at his command, he rallied members of Congress, college professors, conservation groups, and ordinary citizens—and the Forest Service itself—to support a campaign to spare the big trees from loggers. The response was overwhelming. The result was that in 1960, the Forest Service established the 1,240-acre Cooper Creek Scenic Area to protect the big trees and the unspoiled fragment of national forest where they grow. It was, Wharton noted, the first sizeable area of its kind to be established in Georgia. "Once logged," he said, "its original soils disturbed, it would be forever beyond recall, its beautifully organized dynamic system, employing sun energy and the use and reuse of water, air and minerals, damaged beyond repair."

—C. S.

34 Raven Cliff Falls

Spectacular waterfall all but hidden in the earth

My friend Ginger and I had hiked more than two miles on the Raven Cliff Falls Trail without catching even a glimpse of the acclaimed waterfall, considered one of Georgia's most scenic. We were in the sector of Chattahoochee National Forest in North Georgia's White County.

Hiking a waterfall trail in Georgia means winding through curtains of trees, straining for a sight of the main attraction, until the forest finally parts to present the glorious cascade at trail's end.

A two-mile trek with no sign at all seemed almost cruel.

Dodds Creek, issuing from the falls at some point above us, tumbled and rushed beside the trail. On its banks it wore a mossy cloak that glowed green in the day's overcast light, and it sang the ever-changing song of all mountain streams: a descant of trickling notes above the deep bass of water plunging into pools. We saw no sign of the main waterfall, but smaller falls appeared along the way as though to tease us.

The starry flowers of doll's-eyes winked from the undergrowth; the white orbs of its berries would stare eerily later in the season. Deep green drapes of rhododendron, not yet in bloom, billowed along the stream on either side.

With no trees or landmarks visible near Raven Cliff Falls, the green moss on the foreground rocks supplies the sole focal detail in this scene. The lighting was a challenge: black shadows surrounding the water make a sharp contrast with the brightly lit rock face outside the crevice. I included a single climbing figure to draw attention to the foreground, as well as to show the height of the falls.

The trail was gentle, which was fortunate. Ginger was nursing a sprained ankle but had been unable to resist the temptation of a weekend adventure when I called to invite her.

Now we approached what appeared to be the trail's end. Sheer cliffs rose steeply to our left, rounding to form a barricade before us. The falls, which we still could not see, called with a mighty roar, seemingly emanating from a

The vista at the top of the cliffs was dramatic, but color was muted on this gray day. I created drama for this painting with technique alone—describing the cliffs with ink lines, then washing the background and mountain slope with watercolor only. The result is that the detailed forms of the rock take the spotlight without the need for bright color.

great black fissure in the cliff. We made our way down the final steps to face that jagged tear in the earth.

We peered into the dark.

Within a shadowy world, Raven Cliff Falls roared and boomed, a tower of mist and churning foam glimmering under a crack of sunlight from above. Its mighty voice, deep and powerful, echoed and amplified in the twilight chamber. We stood and marveled at this revelation, all but hidden in the earth.

After a few minutes, we surrendered our spot to the hikers waiting after us. Ginger sat on a nearby rock to eat lunch and rub her ankle, while I made the final climb: a haphazard ladder of tree roots that ascended to the top of the cliffs.

The horizon stretched for miles. From the precipice, the forms of the huge rocks below showed plainly. They lay helter-skelter where they had split and tumbled from the cliffs, scattered along the trail like a child's outsized building blocks.

Looking more closely, I could see small specks of color creeping up the trail toward the falls: more hikers, making their way like pilgrims, to the place where the earth was rent asunder, revealing a kind of miracle.

Raven Cliff Falls is the vision that awaits all who make the journey.

—A. L.

Raven Cliff Falls is one of dozens of breathtaking waterfalls in North Georgia, but it has a remarkable geological distinction that makes it different from the others—and a sight to see.

At first glance, its water seems to gush directly from the solid rock of the massive, ninety-foot-high granite slab known as Raven Cliff. (It gets its name from the ravens that once nested on the area's high cliffs.) But a closer look reveals that the water actually is coming from Dodd Creek, a modest mountain stream whose roaring flow drops straight down through a striking vertical fracture in the cliff's rock face. The dramatic geology makes Raven Cliff Falls unlike any other major waterfall in Georgia—and one of the most scenic. The water descends sixty feet through the sharply angled fracture, followed by a twenty-foot drop into a deep, grotto-like pool, then becomes a swirling twenty-foot cascade into raging Dodd Creek.

The fissure in the towering cliff is about fifteen feet wide and known to geologists as a rock joint. Such a fracture in solid rock was caused by powerful geological forces across millions of years. The fracturing not only gives Raven Cliff Falls its superb natural beauty but also makes Dodd Creek one of North Georgia's most beautiful mountain streams. The creek twists, bucks, and tumbles in rip-roaring fashion as it rushes downstream from the falls through a splendid hardwood forest. As one admiring writer describes it in the online Sherpa Guides: "It splashes and winds through the mountain valley with an abundance of whitewater, riffles and pools, moss-covered seepages, and overhanging tangles of laurel." Along its descending course, the cascading creek creates other picturesque waterfalls, though smaller than Raven Cliff Falls. One, Middle Dodd Creek Falls (which drops thirty feet), is majestic and breathtaking enough in its own right to make many visitors think they already have reached Raven Cliff Falls.

A 2.5-mile trail (one way) takes visitors from a parking lot up to Raven Cliff Falls. Hugging Dodd Creek for most of the way, the trail—the bed of a logging road from the early 1900s—is considered one of the best hiking paths in Georgia. Colorful wildflowers grow alongside it in spring and summer among stately hardwoods. About a mile in on the trail, visitors come to the first waterfall of significance, Lower Dodd Creek Falls. Farther up the trail is Middle Dodd Creek Falls.

All this natural splendor and diversity will be protected for future generations to visit within the Chattahoochee National Forest. The falls, the creek and its tributaries, and the trail all lie within the 9,115-acre Raven Cliffs Wilderness Area, established in 1986 according to directives by Congress in the Wilderness Act of 1964. The act created a preservation system for the country's wildest areas and requires federal land management agencies to manage officially designated wilderness in a way that preserves their wilderness character forever. By law federally designated wilderness areas are supposed to be free of human intrusion except for occasional hikers and campers. Power equipment is banned in wilderness areas: no cars, ATVs, chainsaws, or bulldozers.

Today, left alone to let nature take its course, the Raven Cliffs Wilderness Area abounds with mountaintops, a wide variety of ecosystems, rock outcrops, scenic vistas, beautiful mountain streams, and stunning waterfalls—including the unique Raven Cliff Falls.

—C. S.

35 Anna Ruby Falls

A double waterfall spilling from a cliff in the North Georgia forest

Wispy scarves of mist wrap the shoulders of the mountains. They trail in long strands across the road, shrinking the view through my windshield to a circle of twenty feet. I brake and slow when the gray closes in. It's springtime in the Blue Ridge Mountains.

I'm returning home from Asheville after a stay with my artist friend Nan. We showed each other our paintings, as we always do when together, looking for insight from a fresh set of eyes. The stack of watercolor boards makes a loud thump in the back of my van as it pitches to the downhill side of the road. It's a steep ascent to Anna Ruby Falls: I'm making a detour to this Georgia wonder in White County, the last of the great waterfalls on Charlie Seabrook's list I have yet to see.

I join a river of enthusiasts flowing into the trail on this April day. The wonder begins long before the waterfall itself: on the left side of the trail, the creek is a rushing, plunging beauty; to the right, wildflowers call from the trailside, flaunting color and scent in their seduction of passing pollinators. I see wands of starburst foamflower, toothwort spraying blossoms like a sparkler, showy orchis, heuchera, chickweed, violets, and the white-fringed fiddleheads that are just opening.

I am lost in looking, my pace slowed to a crawl. Some hikers walk past briskly, intent on reaching the falls; others linger over the trail's small denizens as I do, heeding the entreaties of each blossom: *Look at me, notice me.*

My life is about seeing—and I have learned that people see different things. Nan travels in a world of luminous color. I imagine her reveling in the jewel greens here that are so intense on this gray day, the silver flash of the water, the pale cool light. She layers slabs of paint with a palette knife or her fingers. I admire her freedom. Nan in turn urges me to paint what I love—to delve into the delicate forms of flower and tree, the vivid moment of the season, to reveal the unique and utter wonder of this place, this day.

OPPOSITE: *The waters of Smith Creek tumble toward the viewer out of the white of the paper, an optical illusion created by the shapes of the greenery and rocks on either side, framing the water and growing lighter as they recede into the distant Anna Ruby Falls and providing the effect of distance. Much of the painting surface is left untouched to mirror the silvery light of the gray spring day. The jewel-like greens of moss and foliage are the only color.*

The mile to the waterfall passes in a blink. Anna Ruby Falls glows on this gray morning, a lacy froth of white over tiers of rock. This is a double waterfall, the child of Curtis Creek and York Creek, which meet here and give birth to Smith Creek—the stream whose path I have followed on this trail.

I step from the paved path to the wooden deck beneath the falls to take photos. Anna Ruby spins a web of water and trees—swirling falls and eddies, a flutter of myriad leaves. What do I see? What is the essential nature of this place? I flash to the waterfall paintings of other artists—the scrolls of Asian painters, the oils of Europe's romanticists. I think, *A thousand artists could stand in this spot, yet each would paint a work unlike any other's.* Van Gogh's world is never mistaken for Vermeer's, nor is Michelangelo's for Monet's.

Other hikers raise their faces to the pounding of the waterfall, each a seeker of beauty painting the canvas of memory with an image of this place at this moment, a picture indelible and lasting like no one else's.

—A. L.

The flowers of toothwort radiate in a delicate starburst against the shadowy log behind them. A muted purple seemed to me to conjure the dusk of the trailside from which these pale beauties nodded, the green of their throats glowing against the shadows of warm rock and earth.

Of Georgia's seven hundred or so waterfalls, the one perennially touted as a "must see" is the enchanting Anna Ruby Falls. Among waterfalls, it is a rarity: it actually consists of two separate waterfalls whose waters dramatically plunge together into a frothy, rocky pool below. Curtis Creek drops an impressive 153 feet; next to it, York Creek, just as spectacular, drops 50 feet. Together, they are called Anna Ruby Falls.

Both streams originate high in the nine-thousand-acre Tray Mountain Wilderness, a vast unspoiled section straddling the crest of the Blue Ridge in the Chattahoochee National Forest. At 4,430 feet, Tray Mountain is Georgia's seventh-highest peak, dominating the southern portion of the rugged wilderness named for it. Such federally designated wilderness areas are pristine roadless landscapes, often forested, where no power equipment is allowed. It all makes for pure water: Anna Ruby Falls has been called a poster site for clean, clear mountain streams flowing out of an untainted wilderness.

Anna Ruby's unusual setting of side-by-side waterfalls helps make it Georgia's best-known waterfall, attracting legions of visitors each year. As the falls plunge in tandem over a gneiss-rock cliff, their waters quickly join together at the bottom, forming a churning whitewater stream known as Smith Creek. Running alongside the creek is an easy, half-mile trail that starts at the visitor center and its adjacent spacious parking lot. A walk up the trail takes visitors to two observation decks for extensive awe-inspiring views of the falls. Perhaps because of its easy walking with the big reward at the end, the paved trail is the most visited hiking trail in the Chattahoochee National Forest. As such, it is also designated a National Recreation Trail.

From the trail, visitors can watch Smith Creek plunge, swirl, and tumble through a dense cove forest within a steep narrow gorge. The forest's natural splendor is rewarding in itself for those who walk the trail. The cove forest is typical of many such ecosystems in North Georgia's Blue Ridge Mountains. Cove forests are biologically rich, hosting all manner of wildflowers, shrubs, and animals as a result of their cool moist environments, fertile soil, and other attributes. Huge tulip poplars and hemlocks dominate Anna Ruby's cove forest; also abundant are oaks, hickories, white pines, maples, and other trees. Below the tree canopies grow evergreen thickets of thick-branched rhododendron and twisted mountain laurel. The tall trees shade Smith Creek's clean clear water, cool enough to support three species of trout—brook, brown, and rainbow. The fish are easy to spot from an observation deck near the visitors center.

As the creek-side trail runs through the cove forest, the tree canopies shade and dapple the footpath. The rhododendron and laurel add a sense of lushness. Along a particularly scenic stretch, acutely angled rock outcrops, cloaked in bright green moss, frame one side of the trail.

About halfway along the trail a rustic bridge crosses the creek, affording close-up views of the rushing stream up- and downstream. Downstream, the creek tumbles over more boulders, forming multiple levels of short cascading waterfalls. From there the stream flows into and forms picturesque Unicoi Lake, the centerpiece of the adjacent Unicoi State Park. (Entrance to the state park and Anna Ruby Falls require separate fees.) The creek continues until it joins with the Chattahoochee River near the town of Helen.

Anna Ruby Falls was named for the last surviving daughter of Captain James Nichols, a Confederate soldier. As a wealthy businessman after the war, he began buying up large amounts of property in the area. In 1869 he acquired the land that included Anna Ruby Falls and present-day Unicoi State Park. Three decades later, heavy logging and poor land management had left huge swaths of the surrounding forest in a state of near ruin. In 1925 the U.S. Forest Service acquired the falls and surrounding land, which was allowed to return to a rich teeming forest. Its natural beauty also came back, giving birth to the Anna Ruby Falls Recreation Area, whose showcase today is the roaring, magnificent twin falls.

—C. S.

Epilogue

My final Georgia wonders trip was a return to McLemore Cove. It was the height of fall color in the Blue Ridge Mountains, and I told Charlie I would love to see the valley from above, surrounded by the mountains while the leaves were blazing.

Charlie recruited a guide. His friend Todd Williams knew of an overlook on Pigeon Mountain. As we wound up the road climbing the mountain, tantalizing glimpses of sky and blue horizon peeped through the trees. It was when we were at the top, scrambling at the edge of the cliffs a thousand feet above the valley, that Charlie stepped through some leaves into a hole.

His leg sank up to his hip, and he fell over, his leg entrapped.

It took him several minutes to extricate himself, with a little assistance from Todd. Miraculously, Charlie was uninjured—and utterly unfazed. He proceeded to the edge of the overlook to take his photographs and exclaim at the view of the valley. Thirty minutes later, he was directing us back down the mountain and across the cove to Lookout Mountain in Zahnd Wildlife Management Area to a view he thought he recalled from a trip years earlier. And once we found it, he clambered out on the rocks at the precipice once again to take his photos.

I hope when my age approaches the vicinity of four score years, I am as curious and engaged in life as Charlie is. As much as any gift in this journey of wonders, his friendship has been perhaps the greatest and most unexpected. What began as an art project, inspired by a list written by a stranger, led to a coauthor, a traveling companion, and a friend.

I had a few other surprises too.

Time. Initially, and naively, I thought of many of these wonders as day trips, with a few weekends needed to cover the coastal islands. A photographer in our kayak group at Okefenokee gave me my first head's-up: when I told him about this project, he advised it would take several years and good planning to capture all these places in ideal settings and seasons. After that I began to build a time line. Spring and fall were the seasons for flowers and foliage, respectively, early morning and late afternoon the best times for light. How many places can you realistically explore and photograph at the height of the wildflower bloom or when waterfalls flow full or when life returns after a burn or when frost paints the leaves?

Water. Some of the wonders are reachable only by boat—Cumberland, Sapelo, and Ossabaw Islands. A half-dozen others are best seen from a canoe, kayak, or raft: Okefenokee Swamp, Ebeneezer Creek, the Flint and Chattooga Rivers, the Altamaha, George Smith State Park. Kayak guides and boat rides became a regular part of these outings, another practice outside my usual routine.

People. In addition to Charlie, perhaps the greatest surprise was learning about the attachments of people to the land. Some of these places are inextricably linked with those who have lived there or whose efforts have ensured their preservation—Sheila Willis and her intimate knowledge of the Okefenokee and Frankie Snow and his dedication to Broxton Rocks.

I returned from visiting McLemore Cove late in an early November afternoon.

I wandered into my small backyard, thinking about the glorious landscape we had seen from the mountaintops. My feet scuffed at leaves drifted high around Georgia asters, which were still their vivid purple. A half-dozen bumblebees, golden with pollen, dipped into the nectar. A small dogwood held out its burgundy leaves. As I meandered, I listened to the small trickle of my water feature, its little pump making a bath for a dozen birds flitting in and out—bright bluebirds, finches, cardinals, a nuthatch. A pair of tufted titmice perched on the rim of the bowl.

I thought of the story Charlie told me during our first meeting, about the research student who traveled to Costa Rica to study hummingbirds. She returned from her journey and found she couldn't name even the most common birds in her Georgia backyard—including the titmouse outside her window.

I looked around my yard. This was not McLemore Cove, a thousand feet in the air, ringed with the flaming colors of the Blue Ridge in fall. Yet it was its own small treasure—a flurry of life and wings and color.

The world is big and wide, and there are numberless wonders on far continents to see.

But it seemed to me, not for the first time, that you can travel the world and return from wondrous sights and then find surprise and wonder close to home, right outside your door.

—A. L.

Afterword

In 1926 an editor at the now-defunct *Atlanta Georgian* newspaper asked Ella May Thornton, then the state librarian, to compile a list of notable natural areas in Georgia. The result was the first list of seven natural wonders of Georgia, under a headline with that wording published in the newspaper on December 26, 1926. State boosters and travel promoters went on to use the list to extol the beauty and splendor of the state. Although Thornton's original list has undergone some revisions in the decades since, many of her picks remain on the current list of some of Georgia's most impressive natural treasures.

In compiling her list of natural wonders, Thornton acknowledged that "there are a number of others of equal rank" that could be on it. We feel the same way: in addition to the thirty-five natural places featured in this book, several other natural areas in Georgia are worth seeing and exploring during one's lifetime. Readers also may have their own picks.

Here's our list of some other natural areas in the state that merit recognition for their beauty and ecological significance:

- Toccoa Falls (Stephens County). At 186 feet, this is one of the highest free-falling waterfalls east of the Mississippi.

- Blackrock Mountain State Park (Rabun County). Georgia's highest state park encompasses some of the most outstanding scenery in the state's Blue Ridge Mountains.
- Vogel State Park (Union County). Georgia's second-oldest state park sits at the base of Blood Mountain in the Chattahoochee National Forest.
- Mount Yonah (White County). Best known for its rock outcrops, its summit offers impressive views of northeastern Georgia.
- Marshall Forest (Floyd County). This is one of few remaining old-growth forests in northwestern Georgia.
- Heggie's Rock (Columbia County). This boasts the best examples in eastern North America of flora native to a granite outcrop.
- Radium Springs (Dougherty County). Its gushing springs were on the original list of Georgia's seven natural wonders. No swimming or fishing permitted.
- Lewis Island Tract (McIntosh County). This is one of Georgia's most extensive bottomland hardwood swamps.
- Wassaw Island (Chatham County). Wassaw is the only Georgia barrier island with an undisturbed forest cover.
- Boneyard Beach, Jekyll Island (Glynn County). The beach and iconic driftwood formed from decades of erosion of coastal maritime forest.
- Banks Lake (Lanier County). This shallow blackwater lake is studded with cypress trees and was formed from the geological phenomenon known as a Carolina bay.
- Lula Falls, Walker County. The falls are often called Georgia's "Little Niagara."

—C. S.

Acknowledgments

I'm grateful for the many people who helped make this book a reality, including the stellar team at University of Georgia Press, the press's director, Lisa Bayer, who expressed immediate enthusiasm when she heard our proposal, and Polly Kummel, our copyeditor.

This book would not exist were it not for my coauthor, Charles Seabrook, who condensed a lifetime of travel and learning into a list that sent me on a seven-year journey. He has been a joy to work with, and his mentoring and friendship have been an unexpected source of happiness.

I owe a large debt of thanks to the teachers and advocates who generously gave their time to accompany me on my visits: Frankie Snow, professor emeritus of South Georgia State College, along with Jim Cottingham, who guided me through the wonders of Broxton Rocks; Jim Cox, biologist for Tall Timbers Research Station, who made sure Charlie and I saw the best of the longleaf pine savannah in the Wade Tract and Greenwood Plantation; John Trussell, who took me, as he has hundreds of others, on a personal tour of Oaky Woods so I could see how special it is; and Tori Phillips of the McLemore Cove Historical Preservation Society, who told us of the cove's historical highlights.

My gratitude also goes to John "Crawfish" Crawford, educator with the University of Georgia Marine Extension and Georgia Sea Grant, who enriched our Ossabaw retreat with a fund of knowledge, and to the Okefenokee native Sheila Willis, who made our three-day kayak trip into that swamp uniquely memorable.

For directions and guidance, I am grateful to Jim Hall of the Pine Mountain Trail Association; Hal Massie of the Georgia Botanical Society, who ensured I made it to the kayak launch on the Flint River in time to see the spider lilies blooming; and Todd Williams, who personally guided Charlie and me to the McLemore Cove overlook on Pigeon Mountain. My son Tyler drove me to the Cooper Creek Scenic Area to find the trail to Valley of the Giants after my two failed attempts.

This project came about partly as a result of my certification as a master naturalist, thanks to Tom Howick, former director of education for the Chattahoochee Nature Center. Tom's program awakened my appreciation for Georgia's amazing natural diversity and introduced me and other students to the experts whose works inform this book, most notably, the late Leslie Edwards, primary author of *The Natural Communities of Georgia*, and Bill Witherspoon, coauthor with Pamela Gore of *Roadside Geology of Georgia*. These two books were among the most-used references for my trips. Tom also introduced me to the practice of nature journaling, which has brought me many hours of enjoyment and enrichment. I also want to thank another educator, Ellen Honeycutt of the Georgia Native Plant Society, who assisted me with plant identification for several sites.

To friends who agreed, at a moment's notice, to accompany me on my travels—Ginger, Jennifer, Celeste, and Amy made these trips a double pleasure. Thank you also to Charna, Diane, Emily, Rebecca, and the artist Debbie Tidwell, who participated in our nature journal retreat. Emily, aka the Kayak

Goddess, made the Flint River expedition a smooth operation instead of a fiasco. My sisters, Jane and Julie, blessed me with visits at opportune times to ensure this book was a family affair. And as a travel companion, I owe most to Yasmin, who always said *yes*. She packed food, chauffeured, conversed with all and sundry we met along the way, and, to boot, was always willing to paddle at the stern of the kayak so I could photograph from the bow.

My lifelong friend and former studio partner, Nan Davis, was unfailingly available for a painting critique, no matter the day or hour, and as a sounding board for any question about how to proceed with a painting when the going got tough.

My parents, Joe and Elizabeth, have my gratitude for their unflagging encouragement in all my creative endeavors. From the time I was a child, they have been my steady cheerleaders and supporters.

I want to thank my sons, Tyler and Joseph, who became de facto art critics, ready to deal me a quick verdict on whether a painting was complete—or what it still lacked. Tyler was especially supportive and enthusiastic.

And to my husband, Michael: We have walked together since we were young. You have always encouraged me to pursue my dreams. I could not have done this without you.

—A. L.

In addition to all the wonderful folks that my coauthor, Ann, has mentioned, I want to thank my wife, Laura, for keeping the home fires burning while I'm out rambling all over Georgia. She's the reason I'm always happy to get back home.

—C. S.